CW00521545

Caroline in the City

About the Author

Louis Chunovic is the author of more than a dozen books, many about show business, including *The Rocky and Bullwinkle Book*, *The Northern Exposure Book*, *The Unseen Bruce Lee*, *Jodie: A Biography* and *Marilyn at Twentieth Century Fox*. He is also a veteran of the Los Angeles-based show business beat, having been, at various times, the Television Editor of *The Hollywood Reporter* newspaper, the Managing Editor of Variety's *On Production* magazine and the on-air Entertainment Reporter for Fox Television in Los Angeles. At the whiskery insistence of Nick and Nora, his longtime beast companions, Mr Chunovic apologizes for not including in the present volume an interview with Tiki, that show business professional who just happens to be a feline and so well plays Salty, Caroline's cat.

Caroline in the City

by **Louis Chunovic**

The official companion to the top TV show

B⧉XTREE

A CHANNEL FOUR BOOK

First published in 1997 by Boxtree, an imprint of
Macmillan Publishers Ltd, 25 Eccleston Place,
London, SW1W 9NF and Basingstoke

Associated companies throughout the world

ISBN 0 7522 1117 X

Copyright © 1997 CBS Inc. All rights reserved.

The right of Louis Chunovic to be identified as the author of this
work has been asserted by him in accordance with the Copyright,
Designs and Patents Act 1988.

All rights reserved. No part of this publication may be
reproduced, stored in or introduced into a retrieval system, or
transmitted, in any form, or by any means (electronic,
mechanical, photocopying, recording or otherwise) without the
prior written permission of the publisher. Any person who does
any unauthorized act in relation to this publication may be liable
to criminal prosecution and civil claims for damage.

1 3 5 7 9 8 6 4 2
A CIP catalogue record for this book is
available from the British Library

Comic strips written by Allen Mogol
and illustrated by Kersten Bros. Studio

Printed by Bath Press

Cover artwork © 1995 CBS Inc. All rights reserved.

This book is sold subject to the condition that it shall not, by way
of trade or otherwise, be lent, re-sold, hired out, or otherwise
circulated without the publisher's prior consent in any form of
binding or cover other than that in which it is published and
without a similar condition including this condition being imposed
on the subsequent purchaser.

contents

part one caroline in the suburbs

part two the cast

part three the episodes

Acknowledgments

My thanks to the creators, cast and crew of *Caroline in the City* for engaging candor and hospitality to an inquisitive stranger, and to Jenny Olivier at Boxtree, Nancy Allen at Marquee Images, Jeffrey Nemerovski at CBS and Christopher Fife at Barron/Pennette for their help and professionalism.

Welcome to the City

Gentle Reader

If you've found your way to this book, you must *really* care for *Caroline in the City*, and that's good enough for me.

I'm a veteran of the L.A.-based show business beat, and I've visited many sets and interviewed many celebrities.

So it's a particular pleasure to tell you all about *Caroline* and its ensemble cast. The show is charming and witty, and they are young and still unspoiled by fame and success. And because I have every faith in your taste in television and your enthusiastic curiosity, I'm going to take you to the *real* Hollywood where the *real* Caroline and Richard and Annie and Charlie and Del and Remo live, and spare you almost all of the usual publicity gush.

I hope you enjoy the visit as much as I've enjoyed bringing you to the show.

Louis Chunovic
Hollywood, California
May 1997

the credits

Lea Thompson *(Back to the Future)* stars in this comedy series about a cartoonist searching Manhattan for love, happiness and some good material for her weekly comic strip. Also starring are **Eric Lutes** *(Frasier)*, **Malcolm Gets** *(Mrs Parker and the Vicious Circle)*, **Amy Pietz** *(Muscle)*, **Andy Lauer** *(21 Jump Street)* and **Tom La Grua** *(The Golden Girls)*.

Each episode of the series is accented with the illustrations of cartoonist **Bonnie Timmons**. The series won an Emmy Award in 1996 for Outstanding Individual Achievement in Graphic Design and Title Sequences.

"The idea for *Caroline* started from a passion, not a deal," says executive producer **Fred Barron**. "We knew the woman we wanted to write about: quirky, engaging, flawed and honest. And both Marco [Pennette] and I were interested in cartoonists, people who could mask their insecurities and express their inner truths with humor."

Caroline in the City is from Barron/Pennette Productions and Three Sisters Entertainment in association with CBS Entertainment Productions. Barron *(Dave's World, The Larry Sanders Show)*, **Marco Pennette** *(Dear John, Dave's World)*, **Dottie Dartland** *(Cybill, Grace Under Fire)* and **Tom Leopold** *(Seinfeld)* are the executive producers.

Premiere: NBC, September 21, 1995
Starring: Lea Thompson, Eric Lutes, Malcolm Gets,
        Amy Pietz, Andy Lauer and Tom La Grua
Executive producers: Fred Barron, Marco Pennette,
              Dottie Dartland and Tom Leopold
Consulting producers: Jeff Abugov, Bill Prady and Donald Todd
Executive consultant: Bob Ellison
Producers: Faye Oshima Belyeu and Bill Masters
Co-producers: Brian Hargrove and Jack Kenny
Staff writer: Cathy Ladman
Directors: James Burrows, Howard Deutch, Gordon Hunt,
       Michael Lembeck, Will Mackenzie and others
Casting: Gilda Stratton, C.S.A.
Production designer: Tho. E. Azzariz
Director of Photography: Richard Brown
Editor: Robert Bramwell
Music: Jonathan Wolff
Cartoonist: Bonnie Timmons
Animation: The Ink Tank
Origination: Studio City, California.
Produced by: Barron/Pennette Entertainment
        in association with CBS Entertainment Productions

part one

Caroline in the suburbs

a day on a hollywood set

The Show and the Stars

C aroline in the City stars Lea Thompson as Caroline Duffy, a Manhattan-based cartoonist who draws on the people and events in her life for inspiration for her successful "Caroline in the City" comic strip.

Those people most prominently include Del Cassidy (played by Eric Lutes), the head of a greeting-card company, and Caroline's sometime boyfriend; Richard Karinsky (Malcolm Gets), a brooding aspiring artist and Caroline's colorist; Annie Spadaro (Amy Pietz), a professional dancer in *Cats* on Broadway and Caroline's spunky best friend and next-door neighbor; Charlie (Andy Lauer), the wigged-out, wisecracking gofer with the sad-puppy face, who skates through life on a pair of rollerblades; and Remo (Tom La Grua), the punctilious owner of the neighborhood Italian restaurant that bears his name. Lots of other interesting people come and go too.

Caroline in the suburbs

Richard obviously is too excited to feed the fish inside the TV

A Hot Set

Like *Seinfeld* and *Friends*, two other popular half-hour comedies set in New York City, *Caroline in the City* actually is filmed in Los Angeles.

Caroline's living-room, the elevator and the hallway in Richard's building and Remo's Italian restaurant all physically co-exist right next to each other, each "standing" set separated from the others only by plywood walls. They can be found inside a single cavernous soundstage on the CBS Studio Center "lot," a venerable suburban L.A. dream factory across from a leafy residential street, where once shows like *Gilligan's Island* were filmed.

The first thing a visitor to the set notices is that the staircase at the back of Caroline's living-room ascends not to some unseen second story, but to a narrow catwalk and a tangle of cables and wires from which sprout down-angled lights and a willowy "boom" microphone.

Caroline in the suburbs

The second thing is that, because of TV's foreshortened perspective, Caroline's living-room and Remo's restaurant both are considerably smaller than they appear on the home screen, and that where their fourth walls would be are only tautly stretched ropes, hung on the middle of which are signs reading:

HOT SET
No Food or Drinks
Thank You

If you step under the rope and look around Caroline's living-room, these are some of the most striking things you'll see.

In one corner, near the framed French-language movie poster, is a fifties-era Emerson console TV set, a big clunky wooden box with a cathode-tube screen. Only where the picture tube should be is an illuminated aquarium, glowing a photogenic watery blue, with real goldfish swimming about inside.

Those are actual pen-and-ink "Caroline in the City" cartoon panels, too, on Richard's side of the mahogany partners' desk, the dominant feature of the living-room. All about are scattered kitschy cat items, from pillows to refrigerator magnets (some of which are pinning snapshots of Lea Thompson and her adorable little kids to the fridge).

On the microwave at the back are *lots* of cat-food boxes – Whiskas brand, mostly. And on a wooden chest near Caroline's comfy green couch is a small pile of videos – what appears to be Caroline's personal collection, including *Reunion, Lily in Winter, My Brother's Keeper* and *My Antonia* – all movies that Richard, more than Del, might want to watch.

It's still quiet on the set at the beginning of this long shooting day. Actors in jeans and tee shirts, scripts in hand, their costumes of the day on hangers thrown over their shoulders, are just arriving. Stagehands are gathering props, "dressing" the sets, loading the cameras, taping camera "marks" on the grey concrete floor or just milling about, exchanging the usual gossip (who's working where, who's sleeping with whom), and, ignoring the signs' admonitions like stagehands everywhere, eating pastries and sipping coffee from Styrofoam cups to help them get started.

On the far side of the ropes are four massive Panavision cameras, each one mounted on a mobile gunmetal-grey cart, each unblinking eye recording a separate aspect of each shot. One camera, for example, might record only a wide shot of the living-room, the second and third might focus in tight close-up on Caroline and Richard, respectively, as they banter back and forth, while the fourth continuously frames the two actors together in a "two shot." This way, when the show is variously assembled by the editor, the director and finally the producers (all of whom put together their "cut," or version, of the episode), there are multiple angles of each "take" from which to choose.

Behind the cameras are the bleachers where, later on that night, an excited audience, several hundred strong, will sit, applauding and laughing as the actors put on their weekly teleplay.

During the shooting season, *Caroline* films once a week, over one long day that stretches from mid-morning to nearly midnight. On shooting day, the cast and the crew first rehearse each scene over and over, blocking out camera moves and positions, sharpening lines of dialogue and bits of physical "business," until finally, after the dinner hour, the audience is brought in and the episode is finally filmed.

Caroline in the suburbs

The Episode

Episode number 223, "Caroline and the Critics," is being filmed one sunny late-March, suburban L.A. day. Directing is veteran TV helmer Will Mackenzie. There are five writer credits for this episode, an unusually large number. They are: Dottie Dartland, Brian Hargrove, Jack Kenny, Tom Leopold and Bill Prady.

The episode, like almost all half-hour situation comedies, is deceptively simple, with "A" and "B" storylines. In the "A" line, Caroline convinces Richard to drive out to Kulawakee Lake, a small town in the New York State hinterlands, to find out why the local newspaper dropped her comic strip. In the "B" story, which takes place mostly at Remo's, Amy (with the connivance of Del, Charlie and Remo) schemes to get back at a dyspeptic critic who's panned her work.

A Work Week in the Dream Factory

Because this is high-stakes, high-pressure American weekly network episodic-series television, during the approximately twenty-six-week shooting season everything proceeds at breakneck speed, with the writers often no more than a single shooting script ahead of the show's actual production schedule and the actors still learning lines that are being rewritten right up to the middle of filming.

By the time the actors deliver those lines in front of the weekly live audience, in the final hours of their fourteen- or fifteen-hour day, and those scenes are committed to celluloid, they will have run through the script approximately ten times. Shooting day ends around midnight. After the weekly shooting day, says Amy Pietz with some understatement, "We're all very tired."

17

Caroline in the suburbs

The following day, usually a Wednesday, the actors come back to work "around noon," she continues, for the first reading of the brand-new script, the so-called "table read," at which the actors, reading from their scripts, try out the dialogue in front of the writers and producers. "We try to sell it really hard and make sure people laugh and the writers look good, so they don't get their jokes cut. [On Thursday] we'll rehearse all day long, then run through for producers." By then, any new sets that have to be built for the week already are up. "They do it really fast. [On Friday] we do the same thing, only more specifically for the networks [i.e., both for CBS, which produces the show, and NBC, which airs it].

"Sometimes [director] Jimmy Burrows will come in, because he owns a piece of the show. It's, like, fifteen or twenty people that will watch the run-through." Then comes the weekend. By this time, both dialogue and plot lines may be substantially changed from the Wednesday script draft, so this is the only real study and memorization time Amy and the other actors get.

That's a particularly crucial factor for Lea, who naturally has the most lines of dialogue in a given episode. Often, between takes of her scenes in the camera-blocking rehearsal, she's off by herself, on a darkened set, still intently studying the script. The weekend is also the best opportunity for behind-the-scenes craftspeople, such as the prop master and the costume designer, to haunt local L.A. shops, looking for that special object or piece of clothing the script calls for. At the rehearsal for camera blocking, usually held on Monday, each of the four cameras' every move is plotted and marked with tape on the stage floor, the levels and angles of a myriad of lights and the levels of microphones are pre-set.

The actors read through their scripts yet again or, if a particular actor is only in a scene's background, a stand-in might be in place. Later, VIPs, such as visiting execs from the network's affiliated stations around the country, might be in for a brief tour, or the actors might have to shoot "promos" for later use.

Shooting Day. They begin to rehearse yet again, at first with scripts in their hands – and they do it again and again – getting soft-spoken suggestions from the director, playing off appreciative laughs from the crew, throwing out suggestions themselves, still fine-tuning lines of dialogue from the "final" script. And then they rehearse some more, going through everything over and over again, right up until 5:30 p.m. dinner call.

Caroline in the suburbs

Then they break, eat, rest, and at seven the audience comes in.

Shooting the half-hour script in front of an audience takes, typically, two to three more hours. And despite the repetition and the down time, the audience members (many of them tourists, including some from as far away as New Zealand and the Philippines) seem to remain fascinated and enthusiastic, helped no doubt in part by the non-stop comedy and patter from Wendee Cole, the warm-up lady (each TV show has a "warm-up" person to get the audience in the mood to respond – to laugh and applaud – though, as the warm-up lady herself points out, all of the others are men). She roams the bleachers tirelessly during breaks in the filming, with her hand-held mike, interviewing tourists, telling jokes and explaining how the shooting will go.

The actors have been rehearsing the script an average of twice a day for a week, but when shooting finally comes, their energies spike upward. "We're happy to be in front of an audience," says Amy Pietz. "Yah! Because we get to show them our little play."

The lights come up on Caroline's loft living-room and Remo's restaurant, and the warm-up lady introduces the cast to rolling ovations of applause:

Tom, amused and gracious, waving in a friendly, but formal, almost old-world way ...

Andy, rollerblading in, a baseball cap pulled down low over his eyes ...

Eric, loping and easy-going, dressed like a Hollywood agent in his taupe silk Del suit, his eyes sparkling with a bemused air ...

Amy, bright-eyed and outgoing; less than two months away from marriage to her long-time boyfriend and a Hawaiian honeymoon, she's radiating good cheer ...

Malcolm, thin and intense, with that tousled look and near bird-like intensity, and finally ...

Lea, high-energy and happy, but intent, too, and so professional ...

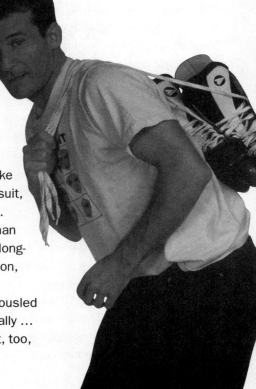

Hours later, after the shooting is done and the audience is gone, it's still not over: there's dialogue "looping" to do, various "pick-up" shots to film, and then the editing and post-production will begin.

The following day, everyone on the production crew is back, doing it all, all over again.

The Second A.D.

"We keep things organized and moving," says the second assistant director of herself and the first A.D., "so we can be most efficient with our time in rehearsal and in filming. We do a lot of the scheduling and the organizing, keeping communication open and everyone informed of what's going on."

She laughs heartily when a visitor suggests that, if a TV production crew is an army, then she's the sergeant. Cindy Potthast's background is theatrical feature films, including *Article 99*, directed by Lea Thompson's filmmaker husband.

How did she get her job? At the Directors Guild hall, she put her name on an "availability list," but a lot of it, she adds, is "contacts." For example, she and the first A.D., the woman for whom she works, were trainees together.

The difference between films and TV? Hours in the day, primarily, she says. On a feature film, each work day is no less than twelve-and-a-half hours long. In multi-camera episodic sitcom television, which *Caroline* is, it "runs more like a play. We have rehearsals three days during the week, the hours are pretty normal, nine to five. We have a day of blocking and sometimes preshooting, that's a twelve-hour day. And then our big shoot day in front of an audience is usually a twelve- to fourteen-hour day. And we present it in front of an audience once a week like a play."

What's the charm of the show? "The cast," she replies without a moment's hesitation. "They're funny and charming and accessible. And they really add to the flavor of the show and what's going on. There's a lot of talent that's very subtle."

Her favorite episode? "The one with the monkeys." The one where, at the very end, you really do see the monkey roaming the streets of Manhattan that Charlie's been ranting about throughout the show; the same episode in which Annie's beautiful but frayed and chain-smoking, pyromaniac friend turns

Caroline in the suburbs

up backstage at one performance of *Cats*. And of course the monkey Charlie's been trying to tell everybody about has a box of matches.

And her hardest moment on the show? Efficient Miss Potthast, who next goes off with a clipboard to the bleachers, where extras are gathering, laughs. "I'm an assistant director," she shrugs. "You have good days and you have bad days."

The Background

In the parlance of television production they are The Background, as in "Cue the Background," an instruction familiar to any A.D.; about fifteen extras, twentysomething girls and boys, all casually dressed, some dragging backpacks or gigantic purses, in which no doubt are copies of their resumés and their eight-by-ten glossies, the true currency of aspiring actors. As is the case invariably on any set, one or two are real stunners, but how well can they communicate through a camera? Do they have that certain something Hollywood has been calling "It" since before the movies learned to talk?

There's an "It" quality about the *Caroline* cast, and an "It" spark about the various relationships – Caroline and Richard and what followed the first-season cliffhanger, Caroline and Annie, Del and Richard, Del and Charlie, and on and on.Looking like students in a particularly fascinating classroom, the extras gather in the bleachers, while the second A.D. sits up on the front railing, consulting her clipboard as she explains their scenes to them and gives out their specific assignments.

First comes the scene in Remo's where Annie Spadaro spots the unpleasant critic who panned her and marches over to his table to throw a glass of wine in his face.

Caroline in the suburbs

"You'll be at Table One drinking coffee," says the second A.D. to one pair. She points to a young woman. "After Amy comes in, go to the phone. That's the 'B' scene. Next comes Denver, 'D' … Is there anyone who has not been placed in the scene yet?" A couple of the extras in the back row raise their hands. "Once you hear Annie, you guys come out and sit in the booth."

Fluffy

The director watches the camera run-through on a large monitor divided into four quadrants, one for each camera's view, with his back to the action. The scene begins with Caroline and Richard, pursued by a barking off-stage dog, dashing up to the wooded front porch of a rural house and bursting unannounced through the front door. There they find Earl, a depressed mechanic, whose wife is about to leave him.

Lea Thompson and Malcolm Gets, not yet made-up, are still carrying their scripts as they practice it. He's wearing his character's shapeless, muddy-brown old man's raincoat, and she has on white jeans, sneakers and a tight, cream-colored tee shirt with short sleeves, so a visitor immediately notices how coltish her thin arms and long legs make her look.

In person, Lea is a classic American Midwestern beauty, with a clear, translucent complexion, big hazel eyes and short, almost-auburn hair. Chewing gum, she's focused behind big-frame eyeglasses nearly the color of her hair. Small evergreens in big pots are set up around the porch, to give the illusion of a surrounding wood, and as Malcolm and Lea continue to practice running past them, she cuts a finger on a rough piece of wood.

Rehearsal momentarily stops and a crew member is there with a bandage almost instantly.

"This is my revenge for cutting down a tree," Lea pronounces, good-naturedly holding up her bandaged finger. "Today the tree spirit got me."

The crew applaud her pluck, then Lea and Malcolm do the scene again.

"Richard, run, run!" Caroline calls out. Chased by the vicious dog, they burst through the shrubbery, run up to the porch and crash through the door.

The crew laugh when, on the barking dog's cue, the assistant director stands in with her loud and fierce *yip-yip-yip*.

Richard pleads with Earl for help with their stranded rental car and the crew behind the cameras laugh again the first time they hear Earl's laconic response:

Caroline in the suburbs

"Pete Seavers is a great mechanic. He's only three miles up the road."

"Great," says Caroline.

"But he's in Albany getting his hand put on."

The line breaks up the guest star, too, every single time he says it. It sounds like a nervous laugh, though, and the director calls a five-minute break, during which he and Lea sit with their visiting actor, amiably chatting about their families, about regional accents and so forth, bringing him in to the TV-show family. When the company returns, the guest star has calmed considerably, but in the interim, the scene's entrance has gotten more chaotic and funnier. It turns out to be a change that Malcolm has suggested; it's a good example of TV sitcom creativity in action. That mean barking dog, which originally didn't even exist in an earlier draft of the script, and then at first had no name, now is called, at Malcolm's inspiration … Fluffy.

Then, at Lea's suggestion, the next time she and Malcolm run in and slam the door behind them, the unseen dog jumps against it, shaking it, while the guest star calls out, "Bad dog! Down! Down!"

As the day wears on, "Fluffy" becomes Fluffy Two, a one-eared pit bull that Earl gave as a present to Wanda, his disaffected wife.

"He ate Fluffy One!" Earl eventually declares with great comic resignation. "Now she's leavin' me, prob'ly gonna take Fluffy with her."

Everyone laughs. And then they do the scene again.

"Quiet, please."

"Scene K, once again."

"Here they come, barging in. And … *Action!*"

And when the scene's rehearsal finally ends, and the four cameras move in a lumbering caravan to set up in another part of the soundstage, someone in the crew starts whistling *The Andy Griffith Show*'s uptempo Mayberry theme.

The Costume Designer

Elizabeth "Libby" Palmer got her start as a cutter/draper for a stage clothier in New York twenty-five years ago. Now, she's *Caroline*'s veteran costume designer and has been with the show from the beginning. Her narrow work space, one wall a well-stocked clothing store for her very particular clientèle, is in a corner of the soundstage.

"In one sentence, my job is to enhance the character through their clothes," she explains.

Caroline in the suburbs

"Caroline is from Wisconsin, that's her base," she says, "so she has sort of a Midwest approach to everything. She's fashionable, but she's not necessarily cutting edge. Her clothes are a little bit more conservative than Annie's. Then you have to take Lea Thompson into consideration in all of this. Lea's very good in classic, simple things, so we try to combine the two."

Richard's trademark thin, flapping raincoat originally came from a costume house, Libby Palmer continues. "He used it on the pilot and he didn't want to part with it." Generally, Richard wears black. "It just sort of suits his soul."

Annie's clothes are "generally body-fitting ... and there's a lot of black because it's New York and also black is a very popular color. She's very, very trendy." But she's also originally from "New Jersey or Queens or one of the suburbs. There's just that little edge of not the top-notch class ... Her leather jacket is a little tougher, whereas Lea's leather jacket is a little sleeker."

The first season, restaurateur Remo was in a "shirt and tie ... Now what we've pretty much done is blazers and sweaters. Much more casual."

One-time greeting-card magnate Del is "much more classic," partly because actor Eric Lutes "wears all these taupey colors really well," Libby adds, pointing to a good stock of silk suits draped on hangers. In the second season, because Del no longer works for his father and has set up his own business, his clothes have gotten more casual, she adds.

When Lea turns up in an episode wearing a miniskirt, looking cute and leggy, that's partly because "all the networks cater to the eighteen-to-thirty-five range, and they'd like the girls to look sexually attractive. That's sort of a given." In real life, because Caroline works at home, "she would probably shlump around in a pair of sweats," Palmer says.

It's a good group, the costume designer says of the actors, echoing the prevailing consensus among the craftspeople. The writers do make changes right up to the last minute, she notes, which "makes it challenging for all the departments to produce quickly."

Dinner

Grumbling about the food is a time-honored show-business tradition. Even on *Caroline*, a visitor overhears two of the extras complain rather whiningly about dinner, though it's hard to imagine why. On their break, cast and crew sit shoulder-to-shoulder at long trestle tables in a low-ceilinged basement meeting-room, which also is where the actors, writers and producers gather for script readings. The walls are unadorned, the servers ladling out dishes are pleasant and competent, greeting many of the crew members by name, and the food is plentiful, hot and tasty. This is the catered menu for one shooting day late in the second season:

Mixed Field of Greens
Chilled Mediterranean Cous Cous
Wheat Baguettes and Butter
Sterling Salmon Bruschetta
Grilled Basil Marinated Chicken
Penne Pasta with a Provocative Arrabiata on the Side
Baked Spinach à la Grecque
Grilled Green Beans, Potatoes and Yams
Handmade Desserts
Iced Tea, Lemonade and Milk
Flat Waters and European Sodas

Caroline in the suburbs

Creating *Caroline*

In the cutthroat competition of primetime television, *Caroline* was an anomaly from the beginning: its writer/producers first developed the concept of the series for CBS, which passed on the concept, then turned around and sold it to arch-rival NBC, where it quickly became a vehicle for Lea Thompson. To this day, though, CBS's in-house production arm, CBS Productions, remains the show's producing "studio" and, eventually, it will be the company that will sell *Caroline* into syndication.

The show's success "has to be something they're proud of and embarrassed by at the same time," says Marco Pennette with a boyish grin. Bright-eyed and apple-cheeked, he created *Caroline in the City* with his partner Fred Barron, who had the original CBS deal.

The two men wrote the pilot "on spec," i.e., on speculation, which is to say without any prior commitments from a studio or network to the idea. Though CBS liked the idea of the show, Pennette recalls, "They said, 'No thanks, we have a lot of female shows in development.'" When the show went over to NBC, the two writer/producers needed a woman's viewpoint and brought in Dottie Dartland (*Cybill*).

"The three of us ended up spending Christmas break at Fred's house, pounding out another version" of *Caroline*, Pennette recalls. The show they had created was about a female cartoonist named Caroline who lives in New York, but it centered on the "odd couple" tension of an older woman/younger man romance. But then NBC's president, Warren Littlefield, gave them Lea Thompson, with whom he'd just made a development deal. "We said great, but if we do a younger man, he's going to have to be twelve, because Lea's so young. So then we said, 'So why else wouldn't they just jump into bed instantly?' And we created Richard based on that. There's enough of an odd couple without the age difference being added."

From there, they assembled the rest of the cast through the auspices of the usual Hollywood magic. Actor David Hyde Pierce, Niles on *Frasier*, is a friend, says Pennette, and he phoned and recommended Eric Lutes, who had just guest-starred as the new gay manager of the radio station where Frasier does his call-in show. "Amy Pietz came in as one of hundreds we were looking at as the next-door neighbor," says Pennette. "We knew as soon as Lea read with her that she was perfect.

"Richard was the hard one." After they'd found no one right in L.A., Pennette was importuned to do a little casting while he was in New York. "Malcolm walked in and I said, 'Do you have any questions about this guy?' And he put on these little glasses and said, 'No, I *am* this guy.'"

Andy (Charlie) originally tested for another role, which was written out of the pilot, Pennette recalls, but because he was so "wonderful and weird," they wrote the messenger character for him and eventually he became a regular part of the show, as did Tom (Remo), whose well-received turn as a restaurant maitre d' in the pilot episode also earned him a permanent spot.

With the second shooting season nearly over and renewal for *Caroline* pretty much a foregone conclusion, Pennette and Barron already are thinking about Season Three. "I'd like the show not to have to go to having Richard and Caroline fall into bed. I think it's almost an easy way out."

So after a second season in which Richard, more or less secretly, pined for Caroline, in Season Three his first love, Julia, joins the show, turning the tension on its head: "It goes from Richard pining for Caroline to Caroline pining for Richard," says Pennette. "I like the triangle among these three characters a lot." Meanwhile, Annie, who has evolved from the "slut next door" in the first

Caroline in the suburbs

two seasons, will get "some real dating stories" in the new season. "We want to keep the show smart and very New York," says Pennette, with "much more subway stuff, much more hanging out in Central Park."

In its first season, airing in the best spot in primetime television, between *Seinfeld* and *ER*, *Caroline in the City* was the number-four-ranked show overall and the highest-ranked new series on any network. Moved in its second season behind *Frasier*, *Caroline*'s biggest competition was ABC's eagerly awaited *Spin City*, ironically starring Michael J. Fox, Lea Thompson's co-star in the *Back to the Future* pictures. The two shows have battled back and forth in the ratings ever since, with *Caroline* holding its own against the *Spin* from the other network's own *City*.

The Directors

Unlike the theatrical-film business, with its autocratic auteurs, series television is a writer/producer's medium. Television directors often are merely hired hands who may be with the production only a week or two, leaving after shooting is completed on a single episode. They construct, at most, an intermediate "cut" of their work, leaving final assemblage to the writer/producers and creators who guide the series week in and week out, while they go on to another assignment, often another episode on another show. They are the journeymen of above-the-line Hollywood.

Of the exceptions to this rule none is more prominent than James Burrows, one of *Caroline*'s major recurring directors. Everyone around in the know tips a hat in his direction – the King, Eric Lutes calls him; he empowers the actors, Lea Thompson declares. His company, Three Sisters, has one of the show's 'A Production Of' credits.

Here's how good the industry thinks Jim Burrows, the multi-award-winning co-creator of *Cheers*, is: the all-important pilot episodes of no fewer than *ten* shows currently on American network television were directed by him, and in the 1996–1997 season, in addition to *Caroline*, he's directed episodes of *Friends*, *Frasier*, *Chicago Sons*, *Men Behaving Badly*, *Pearl* and *Fired Up*. In the conversations with the cast members that follow later, time and again he's saluted for the sensibility he's brought to the show.

For this episode, though, Will Mackenzie, another pro, directs. Affable, with an unruly shock of white hair, he's fit, folksy and readily approachable. He's been doing mostly four-camera half-hour sitcom shoots now for about five years or so, and he watches every angle of every take on his Quad Split four-window monitor, often with his back to the actors on set and the cameras, cackling expansively at the punchlines to all the jokes. He has a good rapport with the cast, with whom he huddles and banters.

A self-described actors' director, the three-time Directors Guild award winner has a familiar face, mostly from his acting days on Broadway and from playing Carol's (Marcia Wallace) husband, Larry, on the original Newhart series, *The Bob Newhart Show*, in the mid-seventies, which is also when he started to direct.

"We got along," he says of how he came to do "seven or eight" *Caroline*s, including his favorite, "Caroline and the Nice Jewish Boy." "All of these actors, you can see, love to rehearse, which is what I like to do. Lea's stage-trained. Malcolm, Amy, they all came from the theater."

He sees his job as making the actors "more comfortable – in their blocking, in their behavior, in some bit of business that they're doing." With their "fourth wall," which is never broken and behind which a live audience sits, four-camera sitcom shoots are like filmed plays, Mackenzie notes. In addition to making his "cut" of the episode, he also makes certain to provide "coverage" – in other words, alternative camera angles and moves and "takes" for the various scenes, so they can be incorporated in the final Pennette/Barron cut of the episode.

"There's a lot of rewriting, right up to the last minute, which I admire. So you see the writers never give up on the material," he says.

The rewriting continues well into the night's filming, after the audience is brought in. The show's writer/producers, including two of the three creators, crowd in front of monitors, watching along with everyone else. If the audience doesn't laugh at a joke, "They'll come up with another joke," says director Mackenzie, "and then they'll change lines on us right there."

The writers will huddle with the director and the actors, while the warm-up lady distracts the audience with quips and a practiced, free-form monologue. Within five or so minutes, they're ready for another take, then it's Quiet on the Set! ... Speed! ... and *Action!*

"The actors are so young and so bright," says Mackenzie, "they can learn it immediately."

Caroline in the suburbs

... And Action!

The lights are down, except those spotlighting a single standing set at a time, while it's being used for the weekly teleplay; the audience is seated in the bleachers, there's a buzz of excitement at the real, live proximity of the sitcom's stars.

Amy, wearing Annie's short black skirt and tough girl leather jacket, greets a friend in the audience – a woman from college, who works for a lawyer to make money, but does theater for children in her free time, Amy says. Then a make-up woman pulls Amy into the light and touches up her face.

Soon, though, Amy is back, strolling over to where Eric is in conversation. "Don't believe a word he says," she advises.

"Hah! She loves me," Eric replies with great mock conviction. Wearing Del's loosely draped silk suit, he delivers the line in Del's character. "If I wasn't married, and she wasn't engaged ... "

"Then what?" she challenges him, just the way Annie would, drawing herself up to her full, feisty height. "Huh?"

It's so self-evident to Del Cassidy: "Once you've dipped your toe in Lutes Lake ... "

Nearby, the writers huddle around the director's Quad Split monitor, anxiously gauging the reaction from real, live TV viewers to their jokes. One of them turns, seeming to take note. Will this banter, too, make it into a future episode?

Their visitor is impressed. "Pretty soon all the writers will have to do is follow you guys around with a pencil and paper," he says, walking away as the two young actors, pleased, and pumped for their performance, prepare to step back into their Remo's restaurant scene.

Meanwhile, Lea, her scene in the living-room with Malcolm finished, walks briskly by, script in hand, trailed by production assistants and the second A.D. "I wonder if they'll get the jokes," she muses as she passes. "They're so weird."

Her question is answered within moments, further down the line of sets, when Caroline and Richard dash madly out of the woods, gasping, through a stranger's front door, pursued by an unseen, ferociously yapping dog.

When the morose stranger reassures Caroline and Richard that it's only Fluffy Two, his one-eared pit bull ("He ate Fluffy One," he replies to Richard's earnest query), the audience erupts into howls of laughter and drumbeats of applause.

The Official Cast Biographies

For the most part, actors' official biographies are the obligatory products of the Hollywood publicity machine and should be regarded with a certain amount of healthy skepticism. Shown theirs, the cast members pronounce them generally accurate, though Amy Pietz, sitting in the back booth on the Remo's restaurant set, calls hers "weird, but certainly no lies" and wants to take a red pencil to it before she thinks better of the idea.

The official bios follow.

LEA THOMPSON as Caroline Duffy

Lea Thompson stars as Caroline Duffy, a cartoonist whose colorful illustrations closely mirror her own life as a successful, single woman living in a beautiful Manhattan loft, in the hit NBC comedy series *Caroline in the City*. Thompson's portrayal of Caroline earned her a People's Choice Award for Best Female in a New Television Series.

Caroline in the City marked the television series debut for Thompson, who has easily made the transition between comedy and drama throughout her career. The Minneapolis native began performing as a ballet dancer, appearing in more than forty-five ballets before moving to New York to pursue an acting career at the age of nineteen.

Perhaps best known for her role as Lorraine McFly in the *Back to the Future* movie trilogy, Thompson made her feature-film debut in *Jaws 3-D*. She then went

on to star opposite Tom Cruise in *All the Right Moves*. Additional feature-film credits include *Article 99*, *Some Kind of Wonderful*, *Dennis the Menace*, *Red Dawn*, *Howard the Duck*, *Space Camp* and *The Beverly Hillbillies*.

Her television work includes roles in the movies *The Substitute Wife* (with Farrah Fawcett) and *Montana*, as well as guest-starring appearances in *Tales From the Crypt* and *Nightbreaker*, for which she earned her first Cable Ace Award nomination.

The Pasadena Playhouse production of *Bus Stop* and the Los Angeles Theater Company production of *The Illusion* are among Thompson's theater credits. Additional theater work includes *The Trip Down Back* at the Actors' Repertory Theater and *Long Time Coming, Carlie Bacon's Family* at the John Drew Theater in East Hampton, among others.

Thompson resides in Los Angeles with her husband, film director Howard Deutch, and their two daughters.

AMY PIETZ as Annie Spadaro

As a child growing up in the Milwaukee suburb of Oakcreek, Wisconsin, Pietz was inspired to become an actress by watching such television legends as Lucille Ball, Carol Burnett and Mary Tyler Moore.

A member of the first graduating class of the Milwaukee High School of the Arts, Pietz went on to study theater at DePaul University, graduating with a B.F.A. in acting. After graduation, she enjoyed the challenges of the Chicago stage, working at such theaters as Steppenwolf, Organic and Eclipse (of which she is a founding member).

After saving up her tips from a

waitressing job, Pietz ventured out to Los Angeles for pilot season and landed a small role on the television series *Star Trek: The Next Generation* and went on to become a regular on the comedy series *Muscle*, where she played the anchor/lesbian Bronwyn Jones.

ERIC LUTES as Del Cassidy

A native of Charlestown, Rhode Island, Eric Lutes became interested in acting when a group of friends encouraged him to audition for a community production of *The Pajama Game* the summer before college. Although he couldn't sing too well, the director cast Lutes because he felt he was physically right for the part.

After that experience he was hooked, and went on to earn a B.F.A degree in acting from the University of Rhode Island. Upon graduating, Lutes headed to Manhattan to pursue an acting career. Unable to support himself by his thespian skills alone, he began working as an office temp and ultimately took a full-time job with a publisher of children's books. Disappointed, but never completely giving up his dream, Lutes returned to Rhode Island, got a job painting houses with his younger brother and eventually started going on commercial auditions in Boston.

At an audition for a bank commercial, he met Christine Romeo, his future wife, where ironically, she was cast to play his wife. Encouraged by his success with commercials in Boston, Lutes decided to return to New York and, soon after, landed his first television role – Mr. Pressman, the manager of the

the cast

Valley Inn on the daytime serial *All My Children.*

Lutes moved from New York to Los Angeles and, shortly thereafter, auditioned for the role on NBC's *Frasier* that would ultimately get him noticed – Tom O'Connor, the new station manager who, Dr Frasier Crane finds out in one of the series' classic scenes, is gay.

MALCOLM GETS as
Richard Karinsky

Immediately after receiving his master's degree from the nation's preeminent acting program, he was cast in the title role of the Marc Blitzstein musical *Juno*, at off-Broadway's Vineyard Theater. From there, he landed the lead in the Mark Lamos-directed *Martin Guerre* at the Hartford Stage Company, in which he co-starred with Judy Kuhn. He then starred in the acclaimed *Hello Again*, with Tony winner Donna Murphy at the Lincoln Center.

Gets was then cast as the lead in the York Theater Company's revival of Stephen Sondheim's classic musical *Merrily We Roll Along*, which garnered him a 1995 Drama Desk nomination as Best Actor in a Musical, as well as an Obie Award. Next, Gets landed the leading role in *Two Gentlemen of Verona* at the Delacorte Theater in Central Court, for which he won the prestigious St. Clair Bayfield Award for Outstanding Classical Performance. He was then chosen to star in the *The Moliere Comedies* at Broadway's Roundabout Theater. The play closed on a Sunday night and on Monday morning, Gets was off to Los Angeles to audition for the part of Richard in *Caroline in the City*.

An accomplished musician, Gets, who once aspired to be a classical pianist, worked his way though college playing piano at rehearsal halls.

ANDY LAUER as Charlie

Emmy-nominated actor Andy Lauer was born in Los Angeles, the youngest of four children. A self-professed former class clown, Lauer says he's "never had a lack of attention in my life."

From ages nine to eleven, he worked extensively as an actor before giving it up for a normal childhood. A gifted athlete, he excelled in football and was the captain of his high school gymnastics team.

Lauer attended San Diego State University but transferred to the University of New Hampshire, where he studied theater arts and history. After college, he backpacked through Europe and then settled in New York

to begin his career. While there, he worked as a busboy at the Friar's Club, where he studied such comedy legends as Red Skelton, Milton Berle, Henny Youngman and Lucille Ball.

In 1987, he returned to Los Angeles and honed his comedic abilities with the improvisational group The Groundlings and with L.A. Connection. Lauer returned to professional acting with a starring role in the film *Never on Tuesday*. He received an Emmy nomination in 1989 for his portrayal of a tough but tender gang member on *21 Jump Street*. His other television credits include *Going to Extremes, Gabby, Matlock, Grand, Murder, She Wrote* and *thirtysomething*. His feature-film credits include the Oliver Stone films *The Doors* and *Born on the Fourth of July*, as well as *For the Boys, Necessary Roughness* and the futuristic thriller *Screamers*.

Lauer lives in Los Angeles. His birthday is June 19.

the cast

TOM LA GRUA as Remo

Tom's La Grua's television career first began to take off when he landed a guest part on the series *The Golden Girls.* Soon after, Tom was cast in a recurring role on the hit *It's a Living* and followed it with the next three years of guesting on numerous different television shows. At this time, Tom reevaluated his career and realized he wanted to do the "big" television series. He then started to achieve that goal when he was cast in the recurring role of straight man "Eddie" on *Home Improvement.* Soon after came spots on *The Jeff Foxworthy Show,* *NYPD Blue, Dream On, Seinfeld, Married ... With Children, Lois and Clark, Platypus Man* and *The Mommies,* where he played three different roles.

Tom is also no stranger to the big screen. His feature-film credits include *Talent for the Game, Disorganized Crime, Big Business* and *Johnny Dangerously.*

Originally from Brooklyn, New York, Tom's acting career began when he joined the Every Man Company – an acting troupe which was led by a monk, Brother John. The Every Man Company, which produced street musicals, was one of the first street theater companies to perform in the Lincoln Theater, where companies from around the world performed. Tom stayed with the Every Man Company from 1971 to 1976, and eventually became artistic director.

In 1974, Tom made his first trip to Hollywood and did a Public Broadcasting System show, *You Can Run But You Can't Hide.* Tom then went back to New York, returning to Hollywood in 1977. In a Peggy Feury acting class Tom met his wife-to-be, Julia, whom he married in 1981.

As a Vietnam veteran, Tom aids vet groups as well as lending his name to Habitat for Humanity. Tom and Julia have three daughters and reside in Los Angeles. In his spare time, Tom enjoys coaching his daughters' softball team.

Conversations with the Cast

When working TV actors in L.A. gather, the talk often is of "pilots" and "pilot season," even of "back-door" pilots, which might be part of a "development deal."

For actors working on weekly sitcom sets there are "through-lines" to ponder, too, as well as "A" stories and "B" stories to rehearse at "run-throughs." Of course, for anyone on a series, perhaps the most eagerly awaited question of all is: "What are you doing on hiatus?"

This is showbiz industry jargon, much of it self-explanatory or simple to understand in context. For instance, the "pilot" is the audition episode, as it were, of a series: If the "suits" at a network like your pilot, it gets the "green light." A "back-door" pilot is a TV movie, or possibly even a "special" episode of an existing series, made with the idea that it might later become the basis of a series on TV, so therefore its principal actors are contractually obligated to continue on in it if the network gives it the go-ahead, i.e., the green light. In a word, they are "attached" to the project. "Hiatus" is the annual summer vacation, when popular TV actors often do movies, thus testing their potential to "cross-over."

The "B" story is the "Meanwhile" story in each individual episode, and that's how it's introduced in the individual episode synopses you'll find elsewhere in this book.

In the interviews that follow, TV lingo such as the above comes easily to the hard-working young actors. The "through-lines" in these conversations are the questions, which are meant to address the very things the actors talk about among themselves.

Lea Thompson

Lea's focused and Lea needs to be. After all, she's Caroline and it's her show. And though she's as young as her principal fellow players, who are just now getting their first tastes of success, Lea Thompson's already had a substantial film career before ever doing TV, and she's married to a film director as well. Unlike some actors, content to just show up and say their lines, she knows all about the business *of show business, too.*

Tiny without seeming to be, skinny and angular, androgynously cute in her off-white tee shirt and jeans, she doesn't appear ever just to stroll around the set; the onetime professional dancer moves gracefully, but purposefully, with a brisk, no-nonsense gait.

She speaks in a soft, unaccented voice, nearly a whisper, seated on the couch in Caroline's living-room, while the rehearsals continue nearby on the Remo's Restaurant set. Then she's called away to rehearse a scene in a car driving down a road, which is shot in another corner of the soundstage, inside a stationary auto. The car is parked in front of a "blue screen," which allows for later electronic "compositing" of the actors in the car with a moving countryside background. Because this is TV, the same car later doubles as a taxi in another scene.

Afterward, during another break, Lea heads for the cluttered quiet of the prop-room. On the way, she grabs a coffee and a Baby Ruth candy bar and, while she sips and munches, the conversation resumes.

She has hazel eyes with a level gaze, auburn hair and extremely fair skin. She seems to be, just as she describes herself, "more produce-orially minded," as well as a "low-maintenance chick."

She's also a babe. Of a particularly clear-eyed and firm-jawed, snub-nosed girl-next-door, all-American sort.

Let's start at the beginning. When was the first time anyone said *Caroline in the City* to you?
Oh, I'd had a development deal with NBC, and I was developing an hour [series] and a comedy.

[Laughing softly]

They didn't really like either of them that I developed, so I got a stack of scripts of all the pilots they were producing, and I read most of them.

Warren Littlefield [the president of NBC Entertainment] called me up and said, "What did you think about *Caroline in the City*?"

I go, "Ah ... "

I'd had the scripts for about two weeks, so I felt really guilty. I said, "To be honest, I haven't read that one." I'd read all the rest of them, but it was the last one in the pile. He said, "That's what I really want you to do. I think it's great." And I felt really guilty, like I didn't do my homework.

So of course I read the script and thought it was really, really sweet, and I loved the whole idea that it was basically, in its heart, a romantic comedy. That's what I loved about it.

Then I met Fred and Marco [two of the show's three creators] and we got along.

[With a small, almost shy smile]

I guess that answers that question.

Yeah, it does. I'd like to hear about what you had in development that they didn't pick up. Tell me about the hour and the half-hour.

The hour was kind of trying to be a little like *Like Water For Chocolate.*

Great movie.

Yeah. It was supposed to be fanciful. Kind of a mystery, but there were fanciful parts of it.

And the half-hour was about a girl who owned a movie theater and kind of projected herself up on the screen in the movies. I bet that would be really interesting.

I know you've been asked this before, but why did you want to do TV?

NBC was really embracing to me. I'd done a movie called *The Substitute Wife*, with Farrah Fawcett, for NBC, and after Warren Littlefield saw the rough cut of it, he called me up immediately and said, "I think you're great in this movie and I'd love to develop something with you. I'd love to have you on NBC, I'd love to make a deal with you." And it was really nice, it was such a nice vote of confidence.

I was just newly pregnant at the time, with my second child, so I thought, I'll do this ...

I didn't think it'd actually come to fruition. I've been around this business long enough to know. First of all, I thought, Well, I could develop it, I don't *have* to do it. And even if I do the pilot, the pilot won't sell. And even if the pilot does sell, the series'll go under. So.

[Rueful little smile]

That's my "optimistic" point of view.

You look like Caroline. What else do you have in common?

Good thing I look like her.

[Small ironic laugh]

Um, I don't know. I'm certainly not as witty as she is.

I always thought if you were the center of the show, it was important to make the character as close to you as possible, close to your essence, not necessarily your life circumstances. That's been the journey the writers and each of the characters and actors have had to make with each other, which is to get in sync with what it is that we do that's funny and that's close to us in a certain way and that services the piece.

[Frowning]

It's hard when you're in the middle of it to know what's the same.

Does Caroline dress the way you do?

No. I'm pretty much of a slob. This [outfit] is me. I'm pretty much, you know, a low-maintenance chick.

Caroline has to be a little more done up and a little bit hipper. Our lives are pretty different ...

How do you become Caroline? Do you put on her clothes?

I don't really become Caroline until the show.

You're not Caroline yet? You weren't Caroline during the run-through?

Not really ...

But that's what the audience does, it puts that special, weird sitcom spin on things, that kind of more up-feeling than you would have if you were doing a movie or if you were a real person.

I get a little more plucky.

[A small laugh]

She's a plucky girl. When we do it [in front of the audience], there's the make-up and the hair and the excitement of it ...

But I do have really specific things with *other* characters that I play.

Like? Give me an example.

Different characters that I've played, I have to have the shoes on, or I have to say a certain phrase to get the accent, or I have to sing a song. I remember when I was doing *Back to the Future*, I'd have to sing "Mister Sandman" before I did it at the beginning of the day.

Why?

Because it was such a goofy song and it would get me in the right mood to be that weird fifties girl.

I sang it so much that they finally put it into the movie.

But with this character, it's different. Each show is different ... with a through-line that I have to find.

What's the through-line in today's episode?

Each show has its problems that you have to solve in terms of making the writing seem more realistic or making you have a strong emotional through-line.

The underlying story is that I want everybody to like me. But you have to do that without being too pathetic and annoying. So I think I'll just put myself into that.

[Chuckles]

That's kind of my exercise for today.

Do you have a favorite moment?

Um, favorite moment? You mean watching it or doing it?

Either one. You pick. Or a favorite episode.

[Wistfully]

Ohhh, I like a lot of 'em.

[A lightbulb goes on]

Yeah, I had this one scene that I did this year with Malcolm where I got drunk. My boyfriend had cheated on me and I got drunk and came to his apartment.

And then passed out.

Yeah, I loved that scene.

What did you like about it?

I thought it was really well-written. And I'd never done a comedy scene where I was really crying, and I did. I was actually really, *really* sad. I was really crying, and I was really telling jokes.

What made you so sad?

Ohhh, that's personal ...

When I'm doing a play, I have to check-in at the beginning of the day to figure out what areas are actually making me feel sad. Sometimes it can be as simple as, I'm tired and I don't want to be here.

And before the play, I'll go through this catalog: what makes me feel bad? So then I can bring it up later when I need to cry. Oddly enough, when it's well-written enough, you don't have to work at all.

Now, don't mistake this, I think this is a very well-written show, but when I read a script, I read a line and it just sits there on the page. But when you guys say it, it's funny. What is that?

Well, that's when you know the writers are getting more confident with you. The first season it was more jokey; now things are more [from] character, 'cause the audience knows us and they have more faith in us.

Is there a feedback process going on with you and the writers? Give me some examples of that.

We listen to each other a lot.

[Adjusting a bandage on her finger]

What did you do to yourself? You okay?

Aw, a tree bit me. A big piece of wood splintered on this post.

[Back to the question at hand]

Um, like Malcolm thought it would be good at the beginning of this scene here if the dog chased us. The writers had written that the dog chased us and then we talked about it: "Oh yeah, that dog chased us here."

So then Malcolm said: "Wouldn't it be better to come into the scene with the dog actually chasing us?" So they rewrote it like that. It was funny …

Sometimes we write "hard" jokes. When [veteran TV director] Jimmy Burrows is here, that's when it's like getting an Academy Award from him if you come up with a hard joke, a joke that really works. That's when he's proudest of you. He trains us to think in terms of how to make things funnier. He empowers the actors … He's got a knack for shaping your ideas.

What do you know about Caroline that someone who's watched every episode doesn't know? Can you give me backstory?

Do you know what? It's very difficult to have a lot of backstory because they change things all the time.

So if you fall madly in love with some piece of backstory, and you go, "Oh, I only have a sister," they'll decide, "No, we have to write a show about your older brother who's gay."

The doctor/astronaut?
Right. And within the show it can change: they set a joke in one show and then that became Richard being Jewish. He was never Jewish until they thought up this one joke. So you have to stay pretty fluid … you [can't] get too compulsive about "This is my character."

You know when things don't look right on you. Certain things don't look right on Caroline.

Give me an example. She couldn't be promiscuous like Annie?
Right. She needs to be nicer than that.

I get away with a lot, and I get away with more this year, but, like, for me to be really mean to people doesn't work. The audience gets dead. If I get in too much jeopardy, if it's just too scary, the audience just goes dead. And that's what's great about an audience: it informs you, you can't fool yourself. They inform you which way the character should go.

What would you like to have Caroline do that she hasn't done yet?
Ummm.

Well, that's part of the fun of it. You're always wondering what they're going to come up with.

I used to be a dancer, so I'd like to do more dancing. That'd be fun.

You know what I'd really like to do? Malcolm and Amy Pietz are *great singers*, and I can sing too. So it would be really fun to do a musical.

A musical episode? Is that something in the works?
You know I think we could do it.

How have Caroline's relationships with the other regulars changed? I mean, it's obvious with Richard and Del.
Right, that changed.

I think they've all gotten richer. I don't think they expected Amy and me to have such good chemistry. I don't think they expected that to work as well as it did. That's grown a lot and I'd like to see that grow even more.

The character of Andy [i.e., Charlie] is really growing a lot this year.

The guest stars that you have on your show: you seem to have an extraordinary number of TV name people. Is that a strategy?
Um, that was a part of the concept of the show, it being *Caroline in the City*, they wanted to bring the city in …

Also, there's a lot of pressure from the network to have stunt casting.

You've been in two of your husband's movies and he's directed two of your

episodes.

I also did a *Tales From the Crypt* for him.

How did you guys meet? Did you meet on the set?

Yes, we met on *Some Kind of Wonderful* ...

Then we fell in love after the movie was over.

How did you get him to do the *Caroline* episodes?

Fred and Marco asked him actually. It made me a little bit nervous, because he'd never done this before, but he's a really good director, so it was fun working with him. He's an actor's director.

What does he say about your work?

He's really pretty supportive. He likes the show.

Does he give you any advice?

A little bit. I really don't want too much from him.

Lea and her husband, director Howard Deutch

[Laughs]

People you love should just say, "You're the best, you're the greatest." I think that's their job.

Does he have any insight-into-the-business advice?

Oh yeah, he comes to it from a different angle, because he started out as an executive and then he became a director.

I see things a little bit more produce-orially than other actors do because of that, living with him for ten years ... like when I think they're wasting money, things like that.

Also, I've been in the business a really, really long time. I think we help each other see what it's like on the other side of the camera.

51

What did you tell him?

Sometimes really obvious things about acting.

Like?

Like the scene's all about sex.

  [Giggles]

  Sometimes simple things are the last to be looked at.

What are you doing on hiatus?

I'm not sure yet. I'm pretty tired. I'm redoing a house. We're building our dream house after ten years, so that's a lot of work. My kids are pretty young, too.

How old are they?

Two and five.

Do they watch Mommy?

A little bit.

Do they get it or are they still too young?

They're pretty sophisticated at five nowadays. She didn't used to like it very much, especially when I kissed somebody else. That really upset her. But I bring her around. I show her things.

  She really doesn't like to watch my movies. She won't watch *Back to the Future.* She won't watch any movie where she thinks something bad is going to happen. It's still too real to her that it's me, even though I explain to her that it's just a character, that it's make-believe.

In one of the earliest episodes you guys made a *Howard the Duck* joke.

I did that on my own. It was supposed to be another movie.

It was very funny, very inside.

The way it was constructed, it was so perfect to make a *Howard the Duck* joke.

When you were a kid in Minneapolis, what did you watch on TV?

I didn't have a TV until I was thirteen, but I do remember watching *Gilligan's Island.* I loved *Gilligan's Island, I Dream of Jeanie.* They were sexy shows. I liked those two shows, and I liked *Hogan's Heroes.* Later it occurred to me, it was *a Prisoners of War camp!* How did that ever happen? They wore swastikas and they were making jokes! Oy!

Did you always want to an actress?

No, I *never* wanted to be an actress.

  [Smiling]

I still don't.

You were a dancer, why did you make the transition? The money?

No. Different reasons. I think basically my body hurt a lot. I was in pain all the time. I had a bad back. And I was also twenty or twenty-one and I hadn't made it; it was such a dead-end road, because there were only a couple of companies in America that were really good at that time ...

I wanted to do something quick, because I always had that feeling that I needed to accomplish a lot, fast. So I just kind of fell into acting.

Is the business what you thought it would be before you were in it? I mean, did you know about the whole myth-making machine?

That whole publicity machine has little to do with what's really going on here. I mean, I don't think people understand how much work it is, how hard it is, which is actually the good news. That's really fun for me, the hard work of it.

When did your day begin today?

In my life?

Yeah.

Six in the morning.

The kids until nine.

Ten when I came here. Then we had a read-through [of the next week's script]. Then we started today.

But it's not just the hours, like, *Boo-hoo, sob-sob!* My life is not that difficult. It's the mental work of trying to figure it out, trying to piece things together, trying to constantly come here week after week and figure out how to make things work better – how to get along with everybody, how to behave. But it's more the mathematical problems in your mind of trying to work things out.

Can you give me an example?

I mean, stringing together a thread. Taking a thread and stringing it through the jokes and through what you know about the relationships between the people and making sense: what time of day it is, what are you eating, where are you going, how cold you are. Stringing all this together requires so much concentration.

At the same time, making the thread loose enough, so you seem like it's effortless, so you're still alive enough to be spontaneous.

Do you have any tricks to do that? Do you meditate, do you work out, eat only vegetables ... ?

I should.

My tricks are more just trying not to mess with my head and stay relaxed and not think too much about it. Like, I can't learn stuff too much ahead of time …

I have to know exactly when to concentrate and when to relax, because if you concentrate all the time you burn yourself out and get too stiff, but you have to concentrate, at that moment when you really have to, and that is like a Zen thing, and it's also an experience thing.

What should the people know who love this show?

The thing that I love about this show … is that I love each and every one of these people here. The actors, I think, are spectacular. I'm constantly surprised each week. I think that's one of the things that makes this show special. Each of the actors is really well-trained, has lots of experience, also is real hungry – a lot of the actors, this is their big chance, you know, their big shot – and they're kind, good people. I feel blessed every day that I come to work …

I feel proud that I helped find them and cast them, and yet I feel in awe of their talent when I'm working with them. They crack me up all the time.

Any advice for them? You're their same age chronologically, but in terms of

experience in the business, you're like their mother.

It's more like, "I know what you're going through, and to have people, all your old friends go, 'Well, you think you're a big star now.'" But you're just really busy, it's not that you've changed.

I know what it's like to have to deal with a business manager for the first time or publicists or what it's like to go on *The Tonight Show*.

I also really feel protective. I want to make sure the show's good, I want to make sure that they all get to do good stuff, and I want to make sure that we stay on top so that we all have jobs for a while ...

We've got people who really love the show. That's a responsibility, and a miracle.

Malcolm Gets

Of all the regulars, wouldn't you know that it's Malcolm Gets who seems in real life the most like his on-camera character?

Even away from the lights, he has the wary intensity that just pours out of Richard when he's on screen.

Maybe it's because Malcolm has just quit smoking, and during a conversation with a visitor he wolfs down a bowl of cold cereal, pronouncing with some determination that he'll take a walk instead of eating when the company breaks for dinner, or maybe it's the speed, that over-amped quality, with which he talks; or maybe it's the gravitas with which he considers each question, no matter how trivial, or that on hiatus he'd like to get back to his first love, the legitimate theater, maybe even do another musical.

It's hard to resist the thought that if Richard Karinsky was an actor who suddenly found himself on television, rather than a frustrated aspiring artist, he'd seem just this same way too.

Tell me what you bring to Richard.

I really love physical comedy, and a lot of the physical stuff initially was mine. Now, they tend to write stuff in the episodes that will allow me do that stuff 'cause I love it.

Like, I don't know if you saw the funeral one, where I cartwheel into the coffin. Stuff like that.

Especially this season, more and more. The episode we read today, there's this thing where I get on a Stair Master. I think they've caught on that I *love* that stuff.

I was a dancer in New York and I *love* physical comedy. So that's something they're catching on to and they give me more and more opportunities.

What else? Anything else that you bring to it?

You know what? It's funny because a lot of the times it's about what I *don't* do as Richard, because I made my living in New York as a singer and a dancer, and so a lot of the times they [i.e., the writer/producers] sort of get wanting to do things like that, so it's about making sure that it's still Richard doing it, and not Malcolm.

[An aside]

I don't know how lucid I'm being today.

[Plunging on]

Again, we're doing another episode today where they want Lea and me to dance, 'cause Lea was a dancer, but we always kinda have to pull back, like [director] Jimmy Burrows or somebody's always coming in, saying, "Um, you have to stay Richard."

What kind of music do you like?

Well, I was a classically trained musician. I started as a pianist and I still do that a lot. God, music's my whole life!

Music's more important to me than acting, I think.

I've done a lot of musical theater in New York, like I worked with Sondheim – three years ago, we did *Merrily We Roll Along* in New York … There's a recording of that. There's, like, three CDs that I'm on.

The kind of music theater that interests me is the more avant-garde stuff … That's probably what I'll do this summer.

What are you going to do?

Well, right now, we're talking about this thing they do in New York in the summers for the last five years called the Encore Series. It's become a big hit, and they do three concerts of older musicals.

They have a big orchestra and they stage them and they bring in really good people. *Chicago*, which is playing on Broadway right now, started as one. They want me to do *The Boys From Syracuse* in May, which would be great. It's an old Rodgers and Hart. And this Bill Finn thing.

Bill Finn wrote *Falsettos* – Bill Finn and James Lapine, who works with Sondheim a lot, they've written a new musical called *A New Brain*, which I did in workshop last summer, and we're going to do a portion of it again this summer and then hopefully do it in New York a year from April, if you can believe that.

So music and the theater are really my first loves. I'm really open to doing films and stuff like that, but I'm very much a person of the theater, and very loyal to it.

In a way, this is like putting on a little play each week.
It is. Absolutely.

Apart from the obvious ways, how has Richard evolved?
That's interesting. Well, I think when we started the show even I didn't realize what a sort of romantic turn we would take with the story.

I had a lot of judgments about what half-hour comedies were before I started to work on one, mostly 'cause I never watched them. I mean, I love *Lucy* and *Mary Tyler Moore* and *Cheers* and those shows, but I never watched TV because I was always on stage at night. And I have to say, I've been really amazed at how much dimension they've tried to bring in and how they've allowed us to bring to it ourselves.

The more I've done the show, the more I find myself thinking that all acting is the same. There's not a certain style [for TV]. You know, if you try to play the jokes, you're dead. All you do is just try to act well.

It's a well-written show, but if you just read the scripts, it's not that funny unless you guys are performing it. What is it that you guys are doing? You're involved in that a lot.
My way of working is trying not to get too self-conscious about that kind of stuff, but I do think that it's about bringing as much humanity to it as possible. In the first season I learned a lot from one of my best friends who watched the show. Early in the first season we did a show, maybe the first one with my mother, and I was concerned that maybe we were getting too heavy, and he – he's in dental school, he works with computers; he's not an actor or somebody

the cast

in show business – [said] to me, "That's the part of the show that I like." He said, "The jokes are easy. You can watch any show and there'll be jokes."
So it's true in a way: the more we've gone on, the more I think all of us are trying to bring as much humanity and genuine feeling into the relationships, the way that you would – I'll try not to get too pretentious, but, the way you would to a Pinter play. And then, the jokes and all that stuff are still going to be there.

Pinter, exactly, because it's something you guys are doing in the silences rather than with the dialogue. I don't know if it's a look or an arched eyebrow or something physical.

I'm always kind of leery about words like "chemistry." I'm always a little cynical about that, because I don't know what it means. "Oh, you guys have chemistry together." But I do think that there's genuine caring amongst this cast, and between the writers. For some reason, it's a willing group, and it's a generous group, and I think that that probably shows somehow.

Even Richard, who is so antagonistic to everybody – somehow all the other actors on the show understand that it's just Richard's defense mechanism.

Tell me something about Richard that we haven't seen on TV.

Wow! I just think he's the total incurable romantic. That's sort of alluded to, but actually we've brought up a lot of stuff about my, of course, dysfunctional childhood and my parents and all that stuff.

You know, I think that deep down he really wants to meet one person and have one relationship, and I think he really wants to be an artist and he wants to create.

At the risk of being pretentious, he's almost the tragic figure on the show.

Whew! My favorite comment that I've heard, from somebody who works on the show – the script supervisor – she told me that one of her friends said that she loved Richard because he was such a loser.

And I liked that because, you know, I've lived a pretty full life and – it's certainly not been a dull life, my life has been pretty crazy – and I'm at that point in my life and my work where I *really* want to say something that reflects that, that I don't feel like somebody who's had an easy life, or a cushy life, or a sanitary life, you know, like most people, I think.

I think people really relate to somebody where things *don't* always work out, somebody who gets evicted, you know, and who gets dumped and all that stuff, 'cause I think that most people in the world feel that way. I certainly do.

The anti-hero.

It's happened to you in real life? You've been evicted, you've been dumped?

[*With a rueful laugh*]

Too many times.

Yeah, before I got *Caroline*, I was teaching to supplement my income, 'cause I was so broke.

What kind of teaching? Music?

Yeah, I was down at NYU.

The irony is, I was in a Broadway play, but you just don't make any money on Broadway nowadays.

Yeah, my apartment in New York doesn't look too dissimilar [from Richard's]. In fact, I think the apartment in the show is bigger than my apartment [in the East Village].

It is.

Do you have a favorite moment or a favorite episode?

There are a few.

I loved the season finale from last year, where I wrote her the letter and I tried to get it back and I got stuck on the ledge. I loved "The Gay Art Show." I thought that one came off beautifully.

There was another one where Sharon Lawrence did a guest spot that I thought was a really rich episode. It had great comedy in it with me and Sharon, where I tried to quit my job –

She was the woman who wanted to keep you?

No, no, it was this one where I quit because Lea was going to get married and I got emotional and I go to an employment agency and I meet Sharon and we end up in bed together and I hide her in the closet. There was a really beautiful scene where I chase Lea out into the rain. It was just a tiny little scene, like from a movie, where it's all about us not saying what we really want to say. I thought that was a really good episode.

If they let you write an episode, is there something you want Richard to do?

Yeah, I have this thing that I joke about, which I call the Bad Soap Opera Episode, which is – *heh-heh, heh-heh-heh* – where I get to play Richard's long-lost twin brother. You know how they do in the soap operas so terribly?

Or, have an episode where Richard starts taking Prozac, and suddenly he's terribly effusive and bubbly, and then the rest of the cast ends up, like, flushing my Prozac down the toilet, 'cause they can't deal with a happy Richard.

the cast

Hopefully that won't be for many years to come.

Are you locked into the show for the entire run?

It depends, you know. I'm trying to take it a day at a time – slow down, see what happens.

The great thing about the show is, there's something really consistent about it that I've never known in the past. I'm used to doing a play for three months and then moving on. And this year I've been much better about sort of giving in to the consistency of this. The hours are like having a regular job. So I do this, then I do other things.

I've started to do a lot more of that this year.

Like what?

Well, I'm back in singing classes.

Have people been talking to you about spin-offs and doing your own series?

Not yet. *Caroline*'s doing well enough and I'm happy to stay here.

Have the bad things about being famous started to kick in yet? Are you bothered by paparazzi?

No.

Have the tabloids bothered you?

No. They've all been pretty respectful so far.

Last year, it was pretty stressful because I wasn't used to it.

I have to say that, most of the time, people are very kind and supportive, and they usually only say something if they're going to say something kind. I do admit that … if you're feeling insecure on a specific day, God knows that's the worse way to go, because then you walk into somewhere and you see a bunch of people talking about you.

I have to admit that my brain doesn't immediately go to *Caroline in the City*; my brain goes to, *Ohmygod! My fly is down!*

But it really has been okay. I think that because I dress differently from Richard, my energy is different from his in a lot of ways, I can still sort of skulk around and people leave me alone.

Richard has a haunted quality. He looks haunted.

[A tentative chuckle]

Ha-ha …

They don't write that in. You brought that to it.

[Sheepish]

Well, I got that from my parents.

[Laughs]

That's funny. Yeah.

Well, do tell.

Oh wow!

[Chuckles]

I think there's a sense of drama to all of my family.

Who are your people?

Oh, I have a fantastic family. I lucked out: I have two wonderful parents who are still together, who love the arts, who always supported me in that, and I have a brother and two sisters.

What's your background?

Both my parents are from London. They're both English. We were raised in the States, the kids.

I think that's the sensibility in Richard – very much so – that I got from my parents. That sort of dry humour.

British?

Absolutely. And that's something of my own that I brought in, which is, my father has that fantastic English humour – very dry, very droll – usually involving how they clean the streets the next day and sweep the bodies up, you know?

A few weeks ago, we did an episode and I wound up making some joke about – the first take they had written something for me like, I said to Lea – I was stuck in this woman's apartment and I didn't want to be there – and I said, "No, it's okay, you go ahead and play with your friends. I'll be fine." And the second take I said something like: "You go ahead. If I'm not here when you get back, look in the freezer for my head."

[Chuckles]

And that I think I got from my father.

What does he do?

He's in publishing.

And my Mom has been a vice principal for eighteen years.

Anything the people who love this show should know?

[An aside]

Wow! What can I say? I don't want to be too sappy.

It really has been really a good experience for me so far. And I came here rather unwillingly, I think. As much as I'd always felt ambitious, I never envisioned my life in California, and I don't know that I thought I'd end up on TV. And the more time that's gone by with the show, the more I've realized how really lucky I am, that – you know, you hear about situations on other shows or temperamental stars or noncooperative writers.

And this show – we all have our moments, believe me – but overall it's been kind of like being in a really great collaborative group the past two years. I hope that translates, 'cause –

[With conviction]

I guess I never really expected it to be as creative as it's been. It has been a really good time. And, this could really be pretentious, but I'm so amazed at how much I've learned about myself from being on the show.

Give me an example.

In other words, I thought that Richard was such a stretch for me at the beginning. I was so happy with myself, because I thought, Oh this is so great because I'm playing this role and *it's nothing like me!*

As I said, over time I've come to realize that there are a lot of things about me like him, and it was really informative for me, in terms of my own personal growth, when I realized, *God, I am really guarded! I am really protected.* And I always thought I was so open and so carefree and all that stuff. I've learned a lot through Richard, which is astonishing. If you had told me three years ago that I was going to say that about being on a half-hour situation comedy, I would've said, "Yeah, well, you're just totally crazy." That's an amazing thing.

I should ask you about playing F. Scott.

That's not such a great story, because I ended up in like two minutes of the movie [*Mrs Parker and the Vicious Circle*], so if anybody wants to see me play F. Scott that's not the one to see.

It was a good experience in that Alan Rudolph [the director] is such a wonderful man, it was an amazing group of young actors and it was a very creative environment in that everybody went off and did their research and then we assembled in Montreal and everybody, like, showed how much research they'd done. And he ended up with a twelve-hour movie, which he cut down to two hours.

So most of what I did in the movie isn't even there. But, you know, again it was a great experience, and I read some – *heh, heh* – great books.

Amy Pietz

"Meet me in Remo's," Amy Pietz says brightly to a soundstage visitor who wants to talk, "in the booth under the sign." Though she's dressed all in black – black leather jacket, long black sweater over black stretch pants and calf-high boots – there's nothing dark or forbidding about Amy. She's too happy, too energetic, too accommodating (offering at one point to find one of the actors, and at another to bring the visitor a cup of coffee) and, even without make-up, far too cute.

Let's start at the beginning: do you remember the first time you heard the words *Caroline in the City?*

Yeah. My fiancé said he had an audition for it. He thought the script was really unique, and something in him said this was going to be a really big hit. He auditioned for the part of Caroline's brother that was cut even before we shot the pilot. That whole storyline was cut.

This is the doctor/astronaut brother who shows up on a later episode when Caroline goes back to her hometown?

Different brother.

[Pausing a beat, reflectively]

I'm sorry, I'm wrong. It was *my* brother, who shows up differently [in a later episode] and is written entirely differently. So he auditioned for that, and they ended up testing *me*, who's very Italian, and they made this whole Italian sort of thing with my family that I don't think was originally there. They didn't really know how they were going to go with Annie.

You're skipping a part. How did it go from your fiancé to you?

I couldn't get an audition.

He's been friends with the network liaison for our show … for about fifteen years. He [the liaison] dated my fiancé's sister, very seriously, for a number of years. And so Kenny was hoping that would help him get the job. He had a call-back [to a second audition], but things didn't go any further and he said, "Amy, there's a part for you. You should try and get an audition."

So I contacted Bob [the liaison] and said, "Bob, I understand this *Caroline in the City* might have a part for me." And he said, "Mmm … I don't really think so."

[She laughs]

Great instinct.

Well, originally they were looking for someone a little older, probably about ten or fifteen years older than me, and maybe an entirely different type. So of course I wasn't right for it at that point.

And then how did you actually get in?

They changed the age of the character, which opened it up for my type, and many other types my age. I auditioned and, um, got it.

Did you have to read something to get the part?

In the pilot episode there's a fruit-throwing scene.

To get the guy.

Yes. And that was what I read for the audition.

So what do you think actually got it for you? Are you a good auditioner or a bad auditioner?

I've had a couple of different agents … The first agency I had thought I was a good auditioner, the second agency I had thought maybe I wasn't. So, I don't know.

How long between when you auditioned and when you got the part?

Umm, about a week and a half. Not too bad. I read a total of three times, then I got the part.

How long before you were on the set, going "Get out!"?

A few more weeks, I believe …

My mother was going through heart surgery at the time. The day that I got the job and had this big audition, she was going in for a triple bypass. I was *very* worried for her.

Where was she?

She's in Milwaukee.

And I was ill. I tend to get the flu or something.

The night before?

Yeah.

[Laughs]

So I really cared more about her life than getting the job. And maybe that helps, I don't know …

Sometimes when you don't place as much importance on it …

When you stop looking at the target …

Yes! Right, right. That's it.

It's like carrying a cup of coffee and not wanting to spill it. You don't look at the cup of coffee, you look straight ahead.

So, what's the difference between you and Annie? You look a lot alike.

[Laughs]

Um, you know I get this comment a lot from people. They think I'm a lot older and when they meet me in person they realize I'm a lot younger than how I play the character. So one thing I've learned from fans or people who watch the show is that Annie's probably a few years older than me.

And, certainly, I'm engaged for a while to my fiancé, so I'm not a promiscuous-type person. Annie, of course, is.

But I used to be.

[Laughs]

I used to play around a lot.

[Giggles]

But probably not to the *brazen* degree that Annie Spadaro has.

Is your fiancé the guy who played Del's usher in the wedding episode?

Uh-huh. He played one of them, one of the guys vying for that. He played the one who was betting on the ponies.

Is there any strain? I mean, you got the job, you're on TV every week and he's not. Do you joke about it or what?

At first we did. I mean, it's really hard being an actor. Every profession is hard these days. It seems like people are working longer hours, everybody's dragged down with all their work. So, you know, it's hard being an unemployed actor looking for work, and going through pilot season and auditions. And that's his journey right now. And that's always been mine. So it's hard to balance that too.

─────────────────────────────

I try to keep his confidence and his ego at a really high level, because that's what books jobs. And he tries to help me through my neuroses and self-doubt and, you know, how much stress and pressure we're under here. So we give and take for each other a lot. And we know that the tables will turn, and this job will be over for me and he will be considered successful for a period of time.

You sound remarkably level-headed about it.

Thank you.

It's not always this way.

[Laughs]

How has your character evolved? Do you have input?

Mm-hm. Yeah.

What have you brought to it? How do you "find" Annie? Do you need to put the clothes on or wear the shoes?

Definitely clothes and shoes. For me it's clothes, shoes, hair and make-up, because I don't wear a lot. Obviously.

And when I get all dolled-up …

Part of the costume is to build me up in my bust–

[Laughs]

And it makes me walk differently. I carry myself differently, and I feel different. Plus she has a bit of an accent. I'm from the Midwest and she's a New Yorker, so I put a little bit of a New York in there.

The Bronx?

Uh-huh. Right. So the voice helps too. Then basically I just try to remember how physical she is and how, because she's an actress, she physicalizes her emotions, rather than holds them in, and verbalizes them in a very succinct manner.

So … I try to feel things in my toes and in my back.

I like to overdo things, probably make it a little bigger than how a non-actor would respond to some situation.

How has she evolved? How is Annie different as Season Two ends than she was in the pilot episode?

Ah! Um, well …

Is she physically different, does she have a different 'do?

My hair changes, like, every week, 'cause –

[Chuckles]

It grows really quickly and I have, like, a hair identity problem or something.

I'm constantly trying to figure out a new hairstyle.

Yeah, new 'dos. Hm, how has she changed?

Last year I would say she might be the type of woman who would wear plastic earrings. This year she's the type of woman who would wear DKNY. She's got a little more slick "NBC Must See TV" in her.

[Laughs with pleasure]

I'm probably a little more slick, y'know?

Do you have a favorite moment or a favorite episode?

My favorite one to do was "Victor/Victoria" ...

I had to pretend to be a man, I had to sing and I had lots of scenes, well-written scenes, and it was a really fun experience for me.

And I got to be the "A" storyline and drive the story. It's a totally different experience than doing one-liners in a dry manner to Caroline or Richard. It's totally different.

Are you a professional singer?

I'm a singer, but I'm not a professional singer. I sang for an Alzheimer's benefit, for seven hundred people, last week. That was the first time I'd sung in a long time.

What did you sing?

This song from *Annie Get Your Gun*.

Do you have a moment in the show that was terrible for you? A line you refused to say or a line that took fifty takes or –

Well, the pilot episode was one of the most terrifying experiences of my life. Professionally, it was the most terrifying experience of my life, because so much rides on the success of the pilot: it could make your future, you could win the lottery, or you could go back to pounding the pavement. So you never feel really settled, even if you do get that job. You don't know if the show's going to do well or not, you don't have your character yet.

I did the fruit-throwing scene. All week long I rehearsed it perfectly well, threw it out the window – and I'm a softball player; I'm like an athlete, I know how to aim a flying object.

[Gulps]

I broke the window during the shooting of the pilot, and I burst into tears. I thought I was going to be fired. Oh-oh-oh!

[Mock tears]

I just lost it.

the cast

What is it about this show? I read the scripts, and they're well-written, but they're not funny. Then the lines get delivered and —

It's life gets put into it! Flesh and tone and color and emphasis and inflection and subtext and meaning and history. Y'know? You can layer all that crap in there.

Okay, then tell me something about Annie that someone who's watched every episode of the show doesn't know.

I think the thing we have yet to see on television, but that I know about Annie, is that she's really, *really* vulnerable, and probably very shy on the inside. And it's layered with all these brassy tones. But I think we have yet to see what makes her go out and fuck everything that walks.

And what is that? Do you know?

Well, y'know, I mean —

 [Chuckles]

  If you want to get all serious … I think it's an insecurity in what she really has to offer as a person. She's insecure that she's not offering enough, so she's going to go that extra mile and offer even more. Know what I mean?

Mm-hm. What would you like her to do in the future that she hasn't had a chance to do yet?

Number one, I would have her do a scene with a man and not be tough as nails. I'd like to see how she really feels in a serious relationship, or have her *really* fall for someone and see how that changes her, or I would like to see tragedy or something … But I know that's not going to propel people to watch a sitcom every week, so I don't expect that.

Well, you never know. What are you going to do on hiatus?

I'm getting married in May, and I have yet to plan fully that wedding [less than two months away]. And I'm doing a movie-of-the-week the day after the honeymoon ends. So, literally, the honeymoon will be over.

Where you guys going?

We're going to Hawaii. We didn't want to put a lot of thought into it. We just wanted a beach.

How long have you been together?

It'll be five years pretty soon. Five years Easter.

Tell me about the movie.

Right now it has this terrible title, which is "A Call For Help." It's the first time I get to star in something.

What's the logline?

What's that?

A logline, that's what you read in *TV Guide*. A one-sentence description, the soundbite version.

Okay, the soundbite version: Amy Pietz stars in "A Call For Help," the story of one woman's struggle to –

[Chuckles]

One woman's struggle –

[Laughs]

To, um, overcome domestic abuse in her past *and* her present.

Must See TV!

[Laughs]

Who else is going to be in it?

Hopefully Kenny Williams, my fiancé, will be in it.

Ah! That would be a very smart move for the publicity.

I think so. And he's a very good actor, and he's perfect for the part. And there's a shower scene that I'm very nervous

about, so it wouldn't be too bad to have my newly wedded husband do that job.

Y'know, this is for the fans, for the people who really love this show. What do you want to tell them? What crossed your mind when you heard a guy was coming that was writing a book?

The first thing that crossed my mind was, "Wow, people actually watch the show enough so that someone's going to write a factual account of it!"

And something that I always want to say to people is that, if there's *ever* a clunker show or a clunker moment, it's not for lack of trying. We try *very* hard, and the writing staff works longer hours than anyone could ever imagine. We try very hard to make people laugh. That's all.

Eric Lutes

His light-colored polo shirt, classic-cut baggy white shorts, sneakers and crew socks give Eric Lutes a preppy, collegiate look. Without a doubt, Hollywood's taken to his natural, easy-going manner. Leaning back in his chair in the small office space that doubles as a dressing-room, he might be a frat boy reminiscing about Spring break, rather than a serious actor explaining how he went from a guest shot on **Frasier** to **Caroline in the City**.

His character has been through an arc of changes in the show's first two seasons, going from ex-boyfriend to betrothed and back again, not to mention losing a job and starting a company, and that's just fine with Eric. In fact, now he's got another unexpected direction in which he'd like Del to go.

Do you remember the first time anyone mentioned *Caroline* to you?
It was my second guest star on *Frasier*.

As the ... ?
Gay station manager. And I was talking to David Hyde Pierce [who plays Frasier's brother], and pilot season was about to start, and he was asking me, "Are you up for any particular pilots?" At the time I was doing a bunch of stuff, reading for things and under consideration for some other projects.

And he said, "Before you commit to anything, you need to know about *Caroline in the City*. My friend Marco Pennette is one of the creators and they really want to use you for this thing." So I thought, "Wow, that's pretty interesting," 'cause I was pretty new to L.A. at the time.

I pretty much moved here and within a month did the *Frasier* thing, which really set the ball rolling. I started working, like, all the time.

Where did you come from?
Originally Rhode Island, but I'd moved here from New York.

So I was in the Green Room at *Frasier* and he told me about *Caroline in the City*.

And then, as pilot season progressed ... four other shows wanted to test me, which was kind of incredible. No one was more surprised than me.

All from *Frasier*?
Well, that's kind of what people saw me as first ... but I'd done a thing on *Ellen* that got a lot of notice too. I played a kind of goofy nerdy boyfriend of hers. We

all know that's a sham now. Probably why it didn't work out.

[Chuckles]

And I did a lot of other guest stars. *Mad About You*, a *Rockford Files* movie, a two-part episode of *The Commish*, up in Vancouver, which was actually what they call a "back-door pilot," which kind of caused a little bit of a problem because I wasn't committed to a five-year contract for *The Commish*, if this back-door pilot went. And I was in Vancouver when they sent the script for *Caroline*.

I guess there's a list of pilots that's published sometime during pilot season and it will have who is attached to it. And so for the back-door pilot of *The Commish* ... there was my name.

Suddenly, the people who were going to test me for these other pilots said, "What's up with Lutes? He's doing a pilot, now he can't test for us." My agent had to, you know, calm their fears.

So it was amazing. I was getting the best of both worlds. After so many years of just struggling in New York and doing regional theater and all that.

To just come here and be turning down more than I'm actually doing was wild.

You read for it and they gave it to you immediately?
No. What happened was I read for it, I met Fred and Marco [two of the three creators of the show], they liked it, had me come back and read for Jimmy Burrows [one Hollywood's most successful and respected TV comedy directors, whose company is one of the show's producers].

I thought "Oh, man, Jimmy Burrows!" and met him briefly.

I thought, "Oh wow, I'm gonna get feedback from the king!" Jimmy Burrows is a great guy ... but he's a man of few words. Just comes in and kind of grunts hello.

[Whistling in silent amazement]

And says, "That's good." I'm, like –

[Shaking his head, astonished]

I thought he was going to steer me or direct me. But that was it.

Do you remember what you read?
Yeah, there was a scene in my office – the original office, which was very upscale. It was a scene that never made it in, where I'm talking to my mother on the telephone and I'm doing all this other stuff ...

It's to show how Del could be kind of a liar in a way. He's lying to his mother,

saying, "I can't believe you didn't get your birthday card. I sent it last week."
I'm like –

[Whispering]

"Get me a birthday card!" All this stuff. And they thought it just made him
too mean, mean-spirited, so that didn't get in. Then, of course, there were a
couple of scenes with Lea, which were when we were trying to figure out
where our relationship is going.

How'd you finally get the part?

[About a month after the first meeting with the two creators of the show] I
booked *Caroline*, did the test deal.

All the suits were there from the network. High pressure …

Two-and-a-half hours, just sitting there [waiting to be called in], trying not to
let it get to me.

I thought, "It's a crazy ride, I'm just gonna do what I do and my worrying
about it is not going to change anything." And it really worked.

After two-and-a-half hours, everyone's pretty much gone in the waiting-room,
and they go, "Okay, Eric we're ready to see you."

I came into a room maybe a little bit bigger than this, fifteen, twenty people
in it. Suits.

Lea and I had developed our thing by then, so it was just easy. We finished at
about seven, seven-thirty, something like that, then my wife and I were reading
a play with some people that night.

By about nine o'clock, nine-thirty, I got the call: "Well, they want ya." I was
just more relieved than anything.

How has Del evolved?

He kind of evolved, and then he devolved a little bit.

The first season Del was very much involved with Caroline. They were on
again and off again. But Del couldn't be too much a pigman, then Caroline
would look like an ass, really. Because why would she be attracted to this
guy?

But you see that Del really has a heart and he would more put his foot in his
mouth and say things that were really off-color or whatever. And to this day,
Del's not really a very good pig.

He's working at being The Man. The He-Man. It's more that Del puts his foot
in his mouth, that he speaks before he thinks. He's not stupid, although he is
obtuse. It does take him a little longer to get things. But he's an educated guy.

I think Del's spoiled and that's kind of made him lazy, and he's had things given to him.

Now, we see him lose the big greeting-card company and he has to start all over again. He's going to have to sell his Porsche to make money, lose all the outer trappings that make him what he thinks he is, 'cause Del is very much a guy of labels and image and all that stuff.

Now that he's not with Caroline, they've made him a little more of that and a little more –

[Pauses]

Misogynist, I guess. A skirtchaser.

What do you bring to him? I mean, you do look like Del. What's the difference?
Well, Del wears make-up.

[Grins]

But what do I bring to it? I bring –

[Sighs]

A non-threatening quality to Del. Because a lot of the stuff that he does and says could make guys not want to be near him, because they would feel too competitive. You know, that guy–guy competition thing could be there. I try to bring enough of me to that so that guys can still like Del, so they identify with him and go, "Oh, man, what a lug!"

Then to make the girls say, "Oh –

[An exasperated tisk]

"He put his foot in his mouth again. He said something that was really stupid. But, you know, he's still a good guy. He's tryin'."

How do you find Del? Do you put on his clothes? Do you have some trick, or don't you need any of that stuff?
I wish I could say there was this incredible process I go into. I pretty much just jump into it.

The writing is so good that you know what the character is, so it would be easy to actually just go and say the words and you'd have Del. What I'm trying to do is bring another layer to him, make Del what is written and also make a quality of honesty to Del.

He has, at times, a naiveté that you don't see in the other characters.

Far be it from me to disagree, but I read the scripts and they're well-written, but they're not funny. They're only funny when you guys say the words. What is that?

I can't speak for the others, but for me, I have a sense of irony that I bring to this. A lot of times what really makes a line funny for Del is that you absolutely have to play it straight. You have to play like he just doesn't get what's going on. As opposed to playing the ba-dum-bum quality of a joke. If you just play it more as if this is a reality to you, you can make *that* funny.

Have you got a favorite moment or episode?

The "Nice Jewish Boy" episode, which was a lot of fun for me. I get to say the Blessing at the table.

[Putting his fingers together, as in prayer]

I do, "Here's the people, open the steeple." Then I go, "And this little finger is you," to the girl. And I couldn't believe they kept it. I thought, Standards and Practices will never let this get by.

That's when Del is at his best. When they write that way for Del, I'm really, really happy, because I think that the whole sex thing, and everybody getting laid, gets old. It really does.

For my part, I like it when Del's put in a situation he's dug himself into. Now, how is he going to get out of here?

I mean, posing as a nice Jewish boy! It was so long, they cut a few scenes, but Del goes to Richard and says, "You're half-Jewish, can't you teach me some Jewish things?"

So Richard agrees if I'll pay for lunch, he'll teach me some Jewish words. And he gives me all this misinformation. So I have these little cheat notes and keep going, "Tomorrow, we can spritzering." That kind of farcical thing where you see Del just sweating, trying to save face and be cool.

What do you know about Del that a regular viewer of the show doesn't know? Is there backstory?

I have my own thing that's going on in my mind: Del is actually very straitlaced and repressed, and is making up for it by trying to be out there.

We've been toying with the idea that Del hardly ever gets "it," and that it's just talk, 'cause he has the flashy car and a lot of money. He gets the bimbos that look great, but there's no substance there. It's easy to get a date with those kind of women, and we always assume that he's taking those women home. Maybe he's actually not.

Maybe Del's pre-*Caroline in the City* life was, maybe, preparing for the ministry.

Something turns him. He gets a taste of the earthly delights and he wants to go crazy with that, so maybe, like, the last episode of the run of the show, Del decides to go back and pursue more heavenly endeavors.

If they let you write an episode, what would you write?

I think there's got to be some deeper connection between Charlie and Del. He's put up with this insane guy all this time. I'd like to explore what that is ... Maybe Del and Charlie find out that all along they've been brothers, or half-brothers, and that's why they have some kind of connection.

I'd like to see more stuff with Del and Richard being the odd couple. We're complete opposite ends of the spectrum, but we each have something that the other needs, which we've done many times, but we're starting to get closer too ... there's mutual respect starting to happen, not that Del is highly respectable.

Is there anything the writers draw from you?

Yeah. They know that, for instance, one of my things that I can do really well are "turns," especially last year when I was with Caroline in the relationship. I would say something, off the cuff, that was really inappropriate and then I would have to cover, as if I really meant it.

[Wide-eyed, hair flying; doing Del]

"I meant it. Of course. That's exactly what I meant."

There was a really good one last year: Caroline's giving advice to Annie about how men *really* are. "They say all this stuff, but deep down they really are sensitive, warm," and this and that.

And I'm behind her, going –

[Scoffs]

"Right."

And she looks at me and I'm –

[Does the fake-sincere Del turn]

"*Right!* Right you are. And let me expound on that."

That's the kind of thing that Del does a lot, that I can do, except I probably do it too in real life.

What's going to happen on hiatus?

I had an offer for a film.

Theatrical?

A feature release. A film version of *Curse of the Mummy*, by Bram Stoker. So it's the lead guy in that, an art-historian/detective. I haven't accepted yet.

Then there's a Penelope Anne Miller movie called *The Family Bloom* ... I play kind of a lounge-lizardy used-car salesman.

We're just waiting to see if I can do both films. And then, some time after ... there's an independent feature in Canada that I'm under consideration for. A real nice, sweet romance kind of comedy, kind of an *Il Postino*.

The people that love this show are going to buy this book. Do you have anything to tell them?

Yeah. I'm not nearly as obtuse and dull as Del is. I think people are always amazed when they find out I do visual art. I'm actually the artist on the show.

Tell me about that.

I have a whole series of pencil drawings of the Civil War, where I do them on really good quality vellum paper and different weight graphite pencils. I try to make them look just like tintypes ...

Also, we all like to do crossword puzzles here.

I noticed a *New York Times* crossword puzzle out on Caroline's apartment set. It was completely filled in.

Yeah. Well, in descending order, the champion is Tom La Grua, who plays Remo, then there's me, and then there's Malcolm. Andy doesn't bother, Amy's not quite as in to it ...

I just thought the readers might like to know. We're a literate bunch here.

Graphite pencil on vellum. Artist: Eric Lutes

Andy Lauer

Andy Lauer really does wear his rollerblades all the time, at least on shooting day. The smooth, poured-concrete floor of the soundstage is a perfect medium for skating, and as the day of rehearsals progresses, more than once his fast-moving figure scoots through the fourth wall, gliding off the set and past the cameras, coming to a graceful turning stop near the director's monitor, for a quick consultation or a check of the camera positions.

He's even got the blades on, along with his equally omnipresent baseball cap, when he leads a visitor into the small, cluttered office space that doubles as his dressing-room.

In person, Andy is thoughtful, laid-back and it's clear that he's a rather dedicated athlete. After all, the writer/producers, who knew a good thing when it skated up to them, put Charlie on rollerblades only because Andy showed up for work one day wearing them.

How much of an athlete is he? On shooting break, he's participating in the annual San Francisco to Los Angeles AIDS Ride, a grueling, week-long bicycle trip of some six hundred kilometers, which raises money for charity. And if that doesn't seem physically active enough, check out his other plan for hiatus.

How long did it take from being a guest star on the first episodes to being made a regular?
My agent said, "You want him to guest star? That's fine, but you gotta pay him regular money, like a regular role." They said, "Alright. We have no idea what we're going to do with him. But we like him, we're going to start writing for him. We'll treat him as a regular."

And I said, "Great! What fun! Let's do it, man! Rock 'n' roll!" It was wide open, a completely wide-open role.

And one day I came here, I was playing a messenger, and I had my rollerblades on, and they went, "Oh! That's great! Can you rollerblade? Will you rollerblade on the show?"

I said sure.

That's how it started?

I've never been off my rollerblades since. Not in one episode.

How's the character evolved? Has the character evolved, or are you stuck on your blades?

Well. Evolution versus being on blades ... ?

I just found my natural birth father [i.e., Charlie's], 'cause I'm adopted, raised by –

I'm not sure. I've got a strong affinity for monkeys. There's a recurring theme. I'm always involved with monkeys.

Charlie's a cross between semiconductor and super-genius. He's pretty out there.

How do you find the character? Just get on your blades?

After two seasons, it's just easy to meld into the guy. There's a lot of Charlie in me, but he's pretty dense. Dense is safe; there's a lot of safety in density. You don't have to know too much, nobody's going to come down on you for forgetting something, or losing something, or saying something rude or wacked-out.

What do you bring to Charlie besides the blades? Do you tell the writers things and it turns up in Charlie?

Heh-heh. Actually, we just had a discussion over scotch ... Charlie was getting a little too stupid. And I said, "Charlie's really very dense, but intelligent."

If there's a conversation and everybody's looking for the author of *The Canterbury Tales*, and they're throwing out names and they're having a fight about it, then out of the blue:

I'll be sitting on a couch, reading *Mad* magazine, and I'll say, "It was Chaucer." I won't look up from my magazine, I won't do anything, and they'll just look at me, like, "Wait a minute, how did you know that?" It doesn't make sense for a character like mine to be intelligent, but that's where the comedy comes in.

Comedy's opposites. It's funny that I know that when I shouldn't know that.

What do you know about Charlie that viewers don't know?

Yeah. He's got a brother that he grew up with.

What else? Do you know any more backstory?

Yeah. Why I'm always always *always* in blades.

Why?

Hah! I can't say, it's coming up next season.

Do you have a favorite moment or episode?

Yeah. When I discover my birth father.

It's just extremely touching.

If they let you write a script, what would you have Charlie do?

Yeah! Go on a date with Caroline!

Heh-heh.

And?

I've got a crush on her. Charlie's got a secret crush on Caroline. But he's just so busy. Charlie actually gets a lot of girls.

Charlie's a man about town?

Women love a little stupidity in their men.

Hah!

What are you going to do on hiatus?

Oh, man!

I'm going to Fiji, then to Australia, then to Indonesia.

Vacation?

No. I know the preeminent shark documentarians for the Discovery Channel. I'm going to be going along with them, diving with Tiger Sharks in Fiji.

There's a butcher, he's been cutting up goats, chickens, whatever they eat in Fiji, and throwing out the bad products, the gizzards and things like that, off the chopping block, out the window and into the ocean. For the last twenty years! And it's become a Tiger Shark feeding ground.

So we're going to dive down there with the Tiger Sharks. Then, on to Australia ... [to] part of the Great Barrier Reef, and we're going to dive with Great Whites.

Is this going to air?

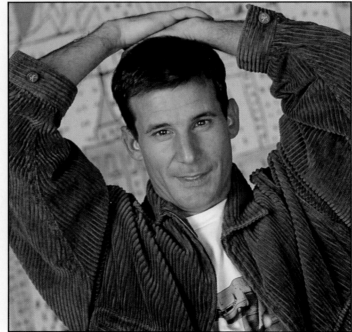

Yeah.

Are you an athlete?

Yeah, I'm a sport.

What else? You dive, blade, bike …

Anything water.

What do you think is the charm of the show?

Our ensemble. All the way, *all the way!* We got a great ensemble.

We're so different, but our problems are similar to the problems other people our age have. They can relate.

We deal with them in a humorous way. And that's what people need to do. Problems are gonna happen, no matter what, so if you can add a little edgy humor in there it's a good idea.

Tom La Grua

In person, Tom La Grua seems earnest, relaxed, personable and professional. He's a veteran TV and film actor – he looks familiar, but maybe you don't know exactly from where – and he attributes his presence as a regular on Caroline *not to theater training, but to plain good luck.*

It's a typically Hollywood take. On the day he filmed a second guest shot after being in the pilot episode, NBC's boyish, carrot-haired, bearded Entertainment President, Warren Littlefield, happened by just in time to catch Tom do his scene. The rest, as you'll see, is showbiz history: the writers rewrote a new scene for Tom right on the spot. Remo the Recurring was on his way, with Tom becoming an official regular at the start of Season Two.

Let's start at the beginning. When was the first time anybody said *Caroline in the City* to you?

When I came in and read for it. When I did the pilot. That was the first time.

What did you read?

One scene where Caroline comes in and sees Del with his new girlfriend and they have an argument. She makes believe she's out with someone, then Richard comes to her rescue.

How did this go from guest star to regular?

They brought me in to work on an episode in which there was one scene at

the cast

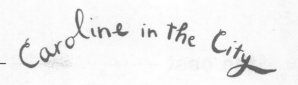

Remo's and a dinner scene in Caroline's apartment. It had happened that Warren Littlefield came down, saw the run-through and said, "Put the dinner scene in the restaurant with Tom. If you have an actor like Tom, you should use him."

It kept going, and in the first season I was brought back twelve times. Then this year, I got a contract to be a contract player on the show.

Would you give me your thumbnail professional biography?

Yes, of course. *Caroline* is my third series. I've done two others. One is *The Famous Teddy Z* for CBS and the second one was *The Boys*, a situation comedy for Showtime. I've done about fifty-five different situation comedies now, since I've been in the business, and over one hundred and thirty episodes of situation and one-hour.

Is there a difference between this and the earlier shows you were in?

They were not just about being funny, but they were also about learning how to do this end of the business, what it takes to do the five days, what it takes to be out on the set, to learn the terminology, all the phrases that are used, and becoming comfortable with that enough so that you can express and be yourself.

And your own background?

I'm Italian-American. I don't speak Italian, but in the show I do, and I use books. I use real phrases. I never say a word in Italian in the show that isn't the truth.

Do you have a favorite moment in the show?

I loved Cigar Night at Remo's. I truly enjoyed getting busted in Amy's apartment with her mother.

How has Remo changed?

Remo keeps changing because the restaurant keeps changing. When we started, the restaurant was an upscale Italian restaurant, and now it's become more of a hang-out place, or a coffee shop for the most part. And with that, he's relaxed into it as well. I don't want to lose his continentalism, or his European outlook on things.

Remo was very much the older school of looking at life on the show, and he's always butting heads with the younger viewpoint.

How do you find the character? Do you need to put on Remo's clothes?

I need to put the clothes on. It's amazing because during the week I can rehearse it and then the clothing comes on. And with that comes the

limitations of when you wear a suit, and the bearing that it gives you is the physical part of the character. I'm a firm believer in the physical part of the character and how he walks, how he holds things, how he behaves when he stands. These are big influences on how you say things.

What do you know about him that a regular viewer wouldn't know?

What we all know is that he's been married once and that he's been separated. What we don't know about Remo is that he had to work at an early age, and it manifests itself now in how hard he works at the restaurant ... He's constantly there. In Remo's life it wasn't always easy. This was the culmination of a life-long dream, the immigrant parents that he comes from as well ... so he's the American Dream.

What did you bring to Remo?

You get an audition, they say, "Come in and read for the part of the Italian maitre d'," every actor in America for the most part is going to come in and give you the stock image.

I had refused to do that. I wanted to find the man who had his own little foibles, who had his obsequiousness, and his desire for money was greater than his loyalty. That's what I brought to the table when I first came.

Is there something you'd like Remo to do that he hasn't yet done?

I would like to see an episode in which we saw Remo's home or his home life.

Tell me about his home life.

He has three children, not unlike myself. They're all grown now, and two of them are out of the house. He still has one at home. And he's not unpopular with the ladies, yet he always has to juggle that with the child who lives at home.

That's why in the episode [in which he sleeps with her mother] he goes to

Amy's house.

Where does he live?

He lives just above the store.

Tell me what the charm of the show is. Why are people tuning in?

The charm of the show is that it's not a pretentious show. I don't think the show tries to be more than it is. And I think they really enjoy that all these characters with all their differences get along.

These are good actors, and I've watched them grow into these roles over the course of the forty-some episodes that we've done. Each of them is now really comfortable within the roles they are playing. You can see that little spark that they bring.

They're a pleasure to act with, because the spontaneity of all of them keeps it fresh all the time.

part
three
the episodes

The episode synopses that follow were originally
written by press agents and others and sent around
to newspapers and magazines, which used them primarily in their daily and
weekly TV listings. Original airdates are for NBC's first run. The synopses are
somewhat revised.

The First Season

The Pilot Episode

Cartoonist Caroline Duffy (Lea Thompson) has her professional life just where she wants it. Her popular newspaper comic strip, "Caroline in the City," has turned into merchandising gold, spinning off greeting cards, books, calendars and other eminently collectible goodies. Perhaps, though, it's just as well that her personal life is far from golden, because it serves as an endless source of material for the strip.

Her outrageous neighbor/best friend Annie Spadaro (Amy Pietz) and her less-than-tactful boyfriend Del Cassidy (Eric Lutes), who also owns a greeting-card company, regularly turn up in the panels of the comic strip, as does everyone from Charlie (Andy Lauer) the gofer to her cat, Salty.

In this series premiere, Caroline hires caustic Richard Karinsky (Malcolm Gets) as her new colorist and breaks up with Del, who promptly announces he's bringing a date to Remo's, their "special" restaurant. After Caroline claims she's got a hot date herself, Annie advises her that landing a date in New York City is as easy as throwing a piece of fruit out the window. One entire fruit salad later, Caroline bops a guy who just could be the new apple of her eye. But he not only turns out to be married, he stands her up at the last minute, too. Richard has no choice but to save her embarrassment by showing up at Remo's and pretending he's the beau. The ploy works just long enough for Del to realize giving up was a mistake.

writers: **Fred Barron, Marco Pennette and Dottie Dartland**
director: **James Burrows**
original airdate: **September 21, 1995**

the episodes

Caroline and the Mugger

Caroline and Del are about to leave for a weekend trip to Atlantic City when a distraught Richard bursts into her apartment. He's been mugged, robbed of not only his wallet but also the portfolio containing Caroline's drawings. Realizing she's got no choice but to stay behind to recreate the work before deadline, Caroline encourages Del to go on without her. When she and Richard spot the mugger on a subway, Caroline takes action; later, she encourages Richard to deal with his trauma and fear of being physically assertive, but taking her advice leads Richard to inadvertently snatch a wallet himself.

writer: **Dottie Dartland**
director: **James Burrows**
airdate: **September 28, 1995**

Caroline and the Gay Art Show

When Caroline and Annie convince gallery owner Kenneth Arabian to consider Richard's paintings for a show, they have no idea that it's for gay artists exclusively.

Richard is delighted to have his *Nude Female Reclining* on the gallery wall, but he can't pretend to be someone he's not, so he's forced to out himself as hetero, even though it's at the cost of losing his first sale, which turns out to have been for twenty *thousand* dollars!

Naturally, Del thinks Richard has lost his mind, but Del learns a thing or two about diversity when he realizes that the men at the gallery don't seem to find him all that attractive.

There's only one snag when Annie encourages Caroline to get a new 'do ... and a new hairdresser: the old one turns up at the gallery's opening night party, where Annie and Caroline's favorite catch phrase (Annie: "Get out!" Caroline: "I'm out!") takes on a whole new meaning.

writer: **Ian Praiser**
director: **James Burrows**
airdate: **October 5, 1995**

Tidbits & Trivia

In "Caroline and the Gay Art Show," and again in "Caroline and the Dearly Departed," Dan Butler plays the gay art-gallery owner. Butler, an "out" gay actor, also appears in Frasier in the recurring role of Bulldog, the obnoxious – and heterosexual – sportscaster. Eric Lutes, who plays Del, also has appeared on Frasier playing the radio station's new, gay manager.

the episodes

Caroline and the Bad Back

The competition between Caroline and Del gets so heated on the racquetball court that Caroline ends up spraining her back. Annie's airy answer to Caroline's agony: a handful of pills that knock Caroline into dreamsville, dulling both her pain and her mind (and giving her a terrible craving for ginger ale).

Meanwhile, Richard and Del scramble to meet Caroline's deadline by finishing her strip for her. Will her nationwide readership find Richard and Del's work funny? Daphne (Jane Leeves) and Niles (David Hyde Pierce), two faithful readers in Seattle, do.

writer: **Bill Prady**
director: **James Burrows**
airdate: **October 12, 1995**

Tidbits & Trivia

The **Caroline/Frasier** *connection continues in "Caroline and the Bad Back," in which Niles and Daphne are briefly seen reading a "Caroline" comic strip.*

Caroline and the ATM

Caroline seems to have a nose for finding embarrassing moments, like this one at her local bank ATM, where a surveillance camera captures her up close, personal (and picking her nose). When the machine fails to spew out her cash, Caroline and Annie march inside, but they can't get the money without giving the bank officials a look at the tape.

Meanwhile, Richard finds himself in girlfriend hell, unable to end his cloying relationship with ditzy, pollyannaish, always-accommodating Shelly (Lauren Graham) without hurting her feelings ... until he tells her he's allergic to her dog.

writers: **Mark Wilding and Jennifer Glickman**
director: **Rod Daniel**
airdate: **October 19, 1995**

the episodes

Caroline and the Folks

Caroline dreads meeting Del's parents for the first time, but it's even worse than she feared when Del and Charlie are trapped on a stalled subway and she must face them alone at Remo's.

Del's mother seems to be a world-class shrew, so Caroline retreats to Remo's kitchen only to end up accidentally dumping an entire bowl of salad all over "Mrs Cassidy," who turns out not to be Del's mother at all.

Meanwhile, Richard's plans for spending a glum thirtieth birthday alone with an appropriately depressing video change when Annie shows up.

Matthew Perry from *Friends* turns up as a guy in the video store who can't take the pressure from Annie's come-on, while Jonathan Silverman from *The Single Guy* series shows up in Remo's as the poor unfortunate meeting his date's unbearably hypercritical mother.

writers: **Fred Barron and Marco Pennette**
director: **James Burrows**
airdate: **November 2, 1995**

Tidbits & Trivia

In the Friends *episode "The One With the Baby on the Bus," which first aired on November 11, 1995, Lea Thompson guest stars as Caroline, who sees Joey (Matt LeBlanc) and Chandler (Matthew Perry) out with a baby and mistakes them for a gay couple. In the* Caroline *episode, "Caroline and the Folks," Perry has a cameo as Chandler, who scurries out of the video store after his I'm-a-sensitive-guy come-on runs into Annie's macho attitude.*

Caroline and the Opera

When Caroline's favorite aunt, Aunt Mary (Jean Stapleton, best known as Edith Bunker on *All in the Family*), visits, she comes bearing Wisconsin cheese and a determination to fix her niece up with a one-time high-school boyfriend (Peter Krause), who is now a successful doctor. At first, Del is delighted to get out of going to the dreaded opera with Caroline, but then he becomes jealous and competitive with the good-looking, hard-driving, multi-lingual doc, even going so far as to take a quick lesson from Richard on the finer points of Italian opera.

Meanwhile, Richard has to fend off girlfriend Shelly's new-age enthusiasms, including her offer of acupuncture.

writers: **Marco Pennette, Fred Barron, Dottie Dartland and Carol Gary**
director: **Tom Cherones**
airdate: **November 9, 1995**

Caroline and the Balloon

The newest giant balloon in the big Thanksgiving Day parade down New York's Fifth Avenue is ... "Caroline in the City"! Now, Caroline can finally live out her childhood dream of being part of the parade. Recruited along with Del, Richard and Shelly as a balloon rope holder, Annie wants no part of getting up at five a.m., until she learns her childhood idol Florence Henderson, mom on the seventies TV sitcom *The Brady Bunch*, will be there.

Meanwhile, Richard has to run for his life when animal-activist Shelly throws paint on a fur coat being worn by a "lady," who turns out to be a very bellicose long-haired man. Later, when they spot the irate, paint-bespattered man, Shelly lets go the giant balloon's rope and flees, setting the Caroline balloon loose and on a collision course with Staten Island.

Florence Henderson, who plays herself, ends up dispensing some very Brady-like motherly advice and reluctantly joins Annie and Caroline for a rendition of the *Brady* theme song.

writer: **Bill Prady**
director: **Tom Cherones**
airdate: **November 16, 1995**

the episodes

Caroline and the Convict

This time it's the real thing: Annie is really head-over-heels for her new boyfriend. When Caroline and Del agree to meet the new boyfriend for dinner at Remo's, they find that Annie's left out one minor detail about his background: he's an ex-convict with a burglary record.

Meanwhile, Caroline encourages Richard to bring in something from home to personalize his workspace, so he shows up the next morning with a gigantic, garish canvas he's titled *My Mother's Womb*, a painting which of course strikes a chord in Del.

Later, when her apartment is burglarized, Annie's new guy is the obvious suspect, but Annie stands by her man ... though only until she spots him trying to make off with Del's prized Porsche.

writers: **Ellen Idelson and Rob Lotterstein**
director: **Rod Daniel**
airdate: **December 7, 1995**

Caroline and the Christmas Break

Caroline and Del plan a romantic Christmas holiday in Paris, but their world-weary travel agent (singer Lorna Luft, whose real-life sister is Liza Minnelli) lays out the facts of booking-a-trip-to-Paris life: no reservations available until April! The proposed delay prompts a bad case of commitment-phobia in Del, and once again Caroline contemplates breaking off their relationship.

Meanwhile, Richard's own thwarted quest to break up with Shelly reaches a desperate stage and he finds himself following Annie's blithe advice to get Charlie to skate over and woo Shelly.

writers: **Michelle Nader and Amy Cohen**
director: **James Burrows**
airdate: **December 14, 1995**

the episodes

Caroline and the Gift

W hen Caroline finds out that the Christmas gift Del gave her, the earrings she didn't like, might have been extremely valuable, she questions his intentions. Annie has questions too, such as, Who's the man from at the New Year's Eve party she can't remember that's calling to confirm the date she can't recall making?

Meanwhile, an excited Richard lands his very first client – a beautiful woman (Fabiana Udenio) who wants him to paint her in the nude as a gift to her boyfriend, who, a nervous Remo confides, is well-connected with the Mob.

writer: **Bill Prady**
director: **James Burrows**
airdate: **January 4, 1996**

Caroline and the Married Man

I t's a fix-up mix-up when Richard, who's vying for the commission to paint a mural, sets Caroline up on a blind date with the art council member (Beau Gravitte) who just happens to hold the key to his future as a successful artist. But when he finds out the man is married, Richard wrestles with a dilemma: protect his friend or further his career?

Meanwhile, Del finds out Caroline is dating again and goes to Annie for advice on how to handle his mixed emotions.

writer: **Wil Calhoun**
director: **Tom Cherones**
airdate: **January 11, 1996**

Caroline and the Twenty-Eight-Pound Walleye

Caroline's proud parents, Margaret and Fred (Mariette Hartley and Earl Holliman), roll out the red carpet when she visits Peshtigo, Wisconsin, her home town, for a ceremony dedicating the Caroline Duffy Park in her honor.

But something smells fishy when her brother Chris, an over-achieving doctor/astronaut who has upstaged her all her life, arrives with a whale of a tale of his own. Caroline, who actually first began doodling as an outlet for her frustration with Chris, and who even keeps a scrapbook filled with how the events in her life have always been upstaged by him, is surprised to learn Chris actually looks up to her.

Fred (Earl Holliman) and Margaret (Mariette Hartley)

Meanwhile, Annie performs a good deed by allowing her understudy a chance to perform in *Cats*, but finds that there may be an ulterior motive behind her colleague's actions.

writers: **Ian Praiser and Carol Gary**
director: **Tom Cherones**
airdate: **January 25, 1996**

the episodes

**"Buddy" and "Sally" from The Dick Van Dyke Show**

Caroline and the Watch

When Caroline and Richard bicker over their shared work space, Caroline purchases an antique "partners' desk." She finds an antique watch inside the desk, and looks up its original owners, writing and life partners Vic Stansky and Stella Dawson (played by Morey Amsterdam and Rose Marie, respectively Buddy and Sally on the original _Dick Van Dyke Show_).

Meanwhile, a guilt-ridden Del attends the funeral of a longtime employee to whom he never gave a raise. But he soon discovers the dead man was a thief.

writer: **Mark Wilding**
director: **James Burrows**
airdate: **February 1, 1996**

YOU DON'T LOOK SO GREAT. HOW WAS YOUR FLIGHT?

THE WORST! I TOOK THE RED-EYE BACK AND IT WAS PACKED!

OH, I HATE THAT! ALL THOSE BODIES SO CLOSE TOGETHER! SO WHO'D YOU SIT NEXT TO?

EVER HAVE SOME STRANGER NOD OFF ON YOUR SHOULDER, AND START SNORING AND DROOLING?

THAT'S DISGUSTING! I'D JUST SHOVE 'EM OFF ME!

WELL, THIS GUY WAS NICE ENOUGH TO WAKE ME UP FIRST.

Caroline and the Bad Date

Annie reintroduces Caroline to the wonderful world of dating by taking her on a manhunt in the wilds of Manhattan. But though Caroline thinks she's picked up the perfect man (Dan Cortese), she later finds out that it's his picture illustrating the dictionary definition of "boring."

Meanwhile, Del convinces Richard to go out on a double date with two beautiful models, but their fragile friendship is sorely tested when the twosome runs into an old girlfriend of Del's who only has eyes for Richard.

writers: **Dottie Dartland and Bill Prady**
director: **Tom Cherones**
airdate: **February 15, 1996**

Caroline and the Proposal

When Del surprises Caroline with a marriage proposal, Richard feels he no longer fits into Caroline's life and decides it's time to look for another job. However, when he walks into the office of a sexy, just-divorced employment counselor (Sharon Lawrence of *NYPD Blue*), he becomes embroiled in a devious plan that spins out of control.

In the meantime, Annie and Remo try to convince a confused Caroline that Richard has feelings for her, and Caroline confronts Richard before giving Del an answer to his proposal.

writers: **Fred Barron, Marco Pennette and Ian Praiser**
director: **James Burrows**
airdate: **February 22, 1996**

Titbits & Trivia

In "Caroline and the Proposal," the part of the employment counselor who beds Richard, played by Sharon Lawrence, was originally written for Kirstie Alley, formerly of Cheers. When Alley couldn't do it, Lawrence was brought in at the last moment. Her guest-star turn was such a success that it led directly to her being offered a starring role in Fired Up, a new weekly half-hour comedy.

Caroline and the Kid

A wealthy man commissions Caroline to draw a bedroom mural for his young son, but when she and Richard arrive on the job, they're faced with a spoiled brat who tries their patience. Meanwhile, Del's competitive nature surfaces when Caroline's handsome ex-boyfriend (Burke Moses) visits.

writers: **Will Calhoun, Bill Masters and Jay Scherick**
director: **Tom Cherones**
airdate: **March 14, 1996**

Caroline and the Ex-Wife

When Del takes Caroline on a spontaneous weekend trip, they run into Del's bitter ex-wife, Jill (Joely Fisher), and her boyfriend, Blair (Kenny Johnson). Del learns that Jill and Blair are engaged, and is thrilled because he can imagine how much better his life will be without the alimony payment. However, after Blair flirts with Caroline, she and Del have to decide whether to protect Jill or their future joint bank account.

   Meanwhile, back in New York, Richard is bombarded by Annie's loud, argumentative family, including her grandfather (Ralph Manza) and her parents, Lou and Angie (Joseph Bologna and Candice Azzara), who are upset that her brother Pete (Adam Ferrara) wants to quit the family funeral home business to become an electrician.

writers: **Amy Cohen and Michelle Nader**
director: **Tom Cherones**
airdate: **March 28, 1996**

Caroline and the Movie

When Caroline and Annie discover a John Landis movie is shooting in their neighborhood, they jump at the chance to become extras, but Annie's already considerable excitement turns to sheer bliss after she learns that her dream man, Robby Benson, is the star of the film. However, Richard doesn't like the idea of Caroline getting an on-screen kiss.

Meanwhile, Del and Charlie try to reclaim Del's Porsche from the Department of Motor Vehicles, only to discover that it's been mistakenly handed over to a compact-car owner who's loath to give the sports car back.

Actor/director Robby Benson and director John Landis (*Animal House*, *The Blues Brothers* and others) play themselves.

writer: **Bill Prady**
director: **Tom Cherones**
airdate: **April 4, 1996**

Caroline and the Cereal

When Caroline's flamboyant agent, James (Meshach Taylor, of *Dave's World*), lands a cereal company deal for "Caroline in the City," Caroline's initial delight and pride sour when she discovers that a pushy corporate executive (Vicki Lewis, of *NewsRadio*) may tarnish Caroline's image with a highly questionable cereal design bearing an unfortunate resemblance to an intimate part of the female anatomy.

Meanwhile, a jittery Del panics as his wedding day approaches and he still doesn't know how to dance, but Annie steps in to help him overcome his fear of stepping out.

writers: **Ian Praiser, Michelle Nader and Amy Cohen (story by Praiser, Nader, Cohen and Robert Lotterstein and Ellen Idelson)**
director: **Pamela Fryman**
airdate: **April 18, 1996**

Caroline and Richard's Mom

Caroline helps Richard confront unresolved issues with his jet-setting mother, Natalie (Elizabeth Ashley, of *Evening Shade*), when she makes a surprise visit to New York.

Natalie, who once promised Richard she would get her personal "friend" Salvador Dali to look at one of his paintings, also tries to impress Caroline with her business connections by introducing her to NBC Entertainment President Warren Littlefield (playing himself in a cameo appearance).

Richard, who's always believed that his mother makes up stories about her relationships with celebrities, discovers that she really did know Dali. Later, when Natalie prepares to move to London, she shows her apartment to a quirky potential renter (John Ratzenberger, of *Cheers*).

writers: **Dottie Dartland and Charles Harper Yates**
director: **James Burrows**
airdate: **April 25, 1996**

Lea, Warren Littlefield, Elizabeth Ashley

the episodes

Caroline and the Bridesmaids

When Caroline entrusts Annie with various maid-of-honor duties, she learns that Annie's strong suits aren't exactly dependability and punctuality, and their friendship strains under the stress of preparing for Caroline's wedding.

Meanwhile, Del discovers that his friends are unreliable, too, and he turns to Richard in his moment of need.

writers: **Will Calhoun and Bill Masters**
director: **Tom Cherones**
airdate: **May 9, 1996**

Tidbits & Trivia

Eric Lutes's real-life wife, Christine Romeo, and Amy Pietz's real-life boyfriend, Kenny Williams, have cameos as a bridesmaid and usher. In May 1997 Amy and Kenny were married in real life.

Caroline and the Wedding

As Caroline and Del's wedding day nears, Caroline is confused and agitated by nerves, reservations and a disturbing dream, while Del experiences panic attacks.

When Caroline and Del's regular priest is called away unexpectedly, a new priest (Michael McKean, of *Saturday Night Live*) takes over, but to Caroline's dismay he is far from a comfort in her hour of need.

Meanwhile, in this season-ending cliffhanger, Richard decides to confess his love to Caroline as a last-ditch effort to stop her from marrying Del, but when he thinks that her fate is sealed, he makes a hasty decision ... to leave town forever.

writer: **Bill Masters**
director: **James Burrows**
airdate: **May 16, 1996**

111

Caroline and the Condom

Caroline has writer's block, leading to reminiscences about Richard's first day on the job, right after she and Del decided that if they were going to resume dating they should go on a "love diet," abstaining from lovemaking for a fortnight and focusing instead on the core of their relationship. But when it looked like they would weaken within the week, she was driven to a desperate search for condoms and an act that could have ruined her reputation and landed her in jail.

Meanwhile, working in Caroline's home creates conflict for Richard over the boundary between his and her personal and professional life.

writers: **Marco Pennette and Fred Barron**
director: **James Burrows**
airdate: **August 5, 1996**

Tidbits & Trivia

This episode, which was one of the first to be produced, was shown out of order and didn't air until after the first season finale cliffhanger.

the episodes

The Second Season

Caroline and the Younger Man

In this second season opener, it's three months after Richard's disappearance and Caroline is thinking about a new assistant. Charlie auditions for the job, but just manages to bat Caroline's cat, Salty, out the window.

Later, Caroline is thrilled when romantic sparks fly between her and Joe (Mark Feuerstein), the emergency-room veterinarian who treats Salty for a minor injury. But her excitement ebbs when she contemplates the age difference between her and her new, younger beau.

Meanwhile, Richard is one sad American in Paris, pining away for Caroline through a series of paintings inspired by his broken heart, so he returns to New York to take a job at an ice-cream parlor, where he just misses seeing Caroline and her vet boyfriend out on a date, which includes raiding a lab that does animal experiments. (One of the other raiders turns out to be Shelly, still carrying a torch for Richard.) The next morning, on her way home after spending the night with Joe, Caroline suddenly runs into Richard.

writers: **Marco Pennette and Fred Barron**
director: **James Burrows**
airdate: **September 17, 1996**

Caroline and the Letter

When Caroline finally discovers that Richard is back in New York, her anger turns into a job offer and Richard must decide if he wants his old position back and to be in Caroline's life again.

Later, Richard realizes that Caroline never saw his love letter, so he schemes to secretly retrieve it. But since his plan involves Charlie, the outcome is chaos, during which Caroline's pregnant friend Vicki (Tia Riebling) goes into early labor, forcing Caroline, Richard and Annie to become instant midwives. Meanwhile, Joe is waiting at Remo's for Caroline, where he and Del meet and get drunk together.

> **Tidbits & Trivia**
>
> *Cathy Ladman, who plays the Elevator Lady in a number of second-season episodes, co-wrote "Caroline and the Letter".*

The next day, when Richard returns to work at Caroline's, he discovers that Annie has copied his love letter, but he convinces her to give him all the copies … or so he thinks.

writers: **Fred Barron, Marco Pennette and Cathy Ladman**
director: **Gordon Hunt**
airdate: **September 24, 1996**

the episodes

Caroline and the Cat Dancer

When Annie finds herself being audited for a year she can barely recall by theater-minded IRS agent Jimmy Callahan (David Hyde Pierce, from *Frasier*, making his second *Caroline* appearance), she misconstrues his friendly manner for amorous intent, but Jimmy has another agenda that makes purr-fect sense to him: an audition for *Cats*, the Broadway perennial on which Annie is a dancer, in return for no more tax problems. So of course Annie sets up the audition ... with Charlie and Del posing as producers.

Meanwhile, Caroline's new boyfriend is frustrated by Caroline's overly friendly relationship with Del, her ex-fiancé.

Elsewhere, Richard is having trouble adjusting to his new apartment where some of his neighbors are considerably less than neighborly.

writers: **Jack Kenny and Brian Hargrove**
director: **Michael Lembeck**
airdate: **October 15, 1996**

the episodes

Caroline and the Guy Who Gets There Too Soon

When Caroline's young boyfriend, Joe, declares his undying love for her, he falls out of favor (and she falls out of a tree). Caroline realizes that she's not ready for the level of commitment that Joe has arrived at so quickly – and callowly – so she decides to cool off the relationship and date a man (Cameron Watson) considerably more mature than Joe. But, surprisingly, she's less than impressed by her date's "adult" manner.

Meanwhile, Richard, who never learned to drive, inherits a classic car from his ninety-year-old aunt, and Del and Annie, who has designs on the car herself, try to teach a very nervous Richard the tricks of driving in New York City.

writer: **Donald Todd**
director: **Gordon Hunt**
airdate: **October 22, 1996**

Caroline and the Dreamers

Richard's dream of being a paid artist finally comes true when he's commissioned by the City of New York to paint a mural. However, his jubilation wanes when he learns that the neighborhood where he's going to paint is one of the most dangerous in the entire city, and he soon finds himself face to face with some local toughs who aren't exactly patrons of the arts. But he wins them over and even paints his masterpiece. There's only one problem, though, which he discovers when the wreckers arrive: he painted his mural on the wrong building.

Meanwhile, Del decides to branch out into more aggressive merchandising, but his dad, the company owner, doesn't see it the same way, so he summarily elevates Del's sister to the presidency, and her first order of business is to fire Del, who is forced to start his own company, with Charlie as his only employee, which forces Caroline to choose between good business and a good friend.

writer: **Bill Prady**
director: **Gordon Hunt**
airdate: **October 29, 1996**

Caroline and the Nice Jewish Boy

When gentile Del falls for Risa Glickman (Rena Sofer, of *General Hospital*), who only dates Jewish men, he takes drastic measures to prove he's of her faith. But that masquerade becomes hard to maintain when he's invited to a Glickman family dinner.

To prove his Jewishness, Del is willing to undergo almost anything, even a covert circumcision, but at the last minute, Risa announces she's eloping ... with a non-Jew.

Meanwhile, Joe, her ardent vet boyfriend, can't be Caroline's date to a posh event, where she will be honored for her comic strip, because one of the event's sponsors violates his principles about animal products. So a very reluctant Richard agrees to be her escort. He and Caroline share a most romantic interlude on the dance floor there, only to face a surprising interruption from ... Joe.

writer: **Tom Leopold**
director: **Will Mackenzie**
airdate: **November 12, 1996**

the episodes

Caroline and Victor/Victoria

Annie takes a reluctant Caroline on a wild ride to Broadway, where she intends to approach Julie Andrews herself and plead for audition as the Oscar winner's understudy in *Victor/Victoria.*

Later, when Annie actually lands the audition, she disguises herself as a man to research her part and inadvertently becomes a threat to Del on the dating scene when she manages to pick up a beautiful woman, who's put off when Annie reveals her deception but won't go through with their date.

Meanwhile, when Richard learns he must have minor surgery for a nasal polyp, Caroline helps him through his panic attacks, but it's Caroline who may need medical attention herself when she hears him utter the "L" word to her just before he goes into the operating-room.

writer: **Bill Masters**
director: **Howard Deutch**
airdate: **November 19, 1996**

Tidbits & Trivia

The director of this episode, in which Julie Andrews is heard but not seen, is film director Howard Deutch (Some Kind of Wonderful, Grumpier Old Men, Article 99, Pretty in Pink and others), who is Lea Thompson's real-life husband. To date, Thompson has starred in two of her husband's films – Some Kind Of Wonderful (1987) and Article 99 (1991).

Caroline and the Comic

When Caroline discovers that Richard's father is a former vaudeville comic, Ben Karinsky (Judd Hirsch, of *Taxi* and *Dear John*, who also starred as Jeff Goldblum's father in *Independence Day*), she tries to reunite the estranged father and son.

After Caroline and Annie view Ben's old act at the Museum of Broadcasting, they talk him into performing for a local charity, where a mid-show glitch promises to bring Ben and Richard closer together.

At the Museum of Broadcasting, Charlie discovers *The Honeymooners*, a classic from TV's Golden Age, and becomes obsessed with Ralph Kramden's goofy neighbor, Ed Norton.

Comedians John Byner and Jack Carter make cameo appearances as themselves.

writers: **Marco Pennette and Fred Barron**
director: **Howard Deutch**
airdate: **November 26, 1996**

Director Howard Deutch on set

the episodes

Caroline and the Therapist

When Caroline observes that Salty, her pet cat, is troubled, she consults Joe, her veterinarian boyfriend, who suggests taking Salty to an eccentric cat therapist, Alicia Crawford-Lane (Valerie Mahaffey, of *Northern Exposure* and *Wings*), who decides that Salty's problem is ... Richard.

Later, Caroline locates Richard's old elementary-school teacher, Mrs Fox (Renee Taylor, of *The Nanny*), in an effort to get to the heart of Richard's fear of animals.

Elsewhere, Del and Charlie come up all wet when their search for true love (or at least a date) unfolds at the local laundromat, while Annie tries to appease her mother, who is vigilantly determined to set her up on a blind date with a forest ranger (W. Earl Brown).

writer: **Tom Leopold**
director: **Gordon Hunt**
airdate: **December 3, 1996**

Caroline and the Red Sauce

It's a recipe for chaos when Annie's mother shows up on her doorstep, suitcase in hand. Caroline soon finds herself in the middle of a mother–daughter war and discovers that this is the least of Annie's troubles when it comes to battling relatives: Annie's father claims to be in love with another woman.

Meanwhile, Richard tries to make a little extra holiday money by working in a department store as a gift wrapper, but his new job turns surreal when he misplaces a difficult customer's special gift and gets demoted to Santa's elf.

Elsewhere, Del has his hands full at their office when Charlie hires a new secretary (Suzanne Cryer) without thoroughly checking her references. But then again, Del can't check her references either … because they're all dead. Uh-oh, have they hired a murderer?

writer: **Bill Prady**
director: **James Burrows**
airdate: **December 10, 1996**

the episodes

Caroline and the Freight King

Another side of Caroline's artistic expression – her childhood dream of becoming a ballerina – is revealed when she's locked in a laundromat overnight with a homeless man (Harry Groener, of *Mad About You*).

Meanwhile, Richard accidentally shows a doodle to Del, who believes that Richard could become a new cartoon talent, which forces Richard into a struggle with his artistic soul.

Elsewhere, Annie is struggling with her superstition, finding herself haunted by a returning five-dollar bill, with the word "Repent" written on it, which she sees as a terrible omen, while Del finally hires a stripper as his new receptionist.

writer: **Donald Todd**
director: **Gordon Hunt**
airdate: **December 17, 1996**

Caroline and the Perfect Record

Caroline and Joe's romance has been running hot and cold, and it heats up when he asks her to spend the night, but it's definitely on its way back into the deep freeze when his ex-girlfriend Lisa (Rebecca Cross) returns from her Greenpeace mission and seeks shelter at his apartment, which turns out not to be Joe's apartment after all.

Later, when a drunk and despondent Caroline shows up at Richard's, looking for a sympathetic shoulder to cry on, he finds himself torn between his strongest instincts and the demands of chivalry.

Meanwhile, Annie is livid when her "perfect record" of never being stood up seems in jeopardy. But it turns out her wayward date has a good excuse: he's dead.

writer: **Dottie Dartland**
director: **Michael Zinberg**
airdate: **January 7, 1997**

Caroline and the Singer

When Annie's sister Donna (Mackenzie Phillips, of *One Day at a Time*), a former pop star, visits New York in hopes of resurrecting her fading career, she finds the love letter Richard once sent to Caroline (who never received it and knows nothing about its existence) and decides that setting the lyrics to music could make it her next big hit single, leaving both Richard and Annie (who's been using the letter to blackmail Richard into tending to her mother) feeling more than a little off-key.

Annie's sister sings

Meanwhile, it's fashion versus passion when Caroline struggles over whether to call her ex-boyfriend, Joe the vet, to retrieve her favorite pair of shoes. She resolves the issue by sneaking into his apartment, where she's promptly discovered.

Elsewhere, Del and Charlie are struggling to get to an important meeting, but they're caught in a midwinter Manhattan blizzard and they're stuck inside Del's Porsche.

writers: **Jack Kenny and Brian Hargrove**
director: **Will Mackenzie**
airdate: **January 14, 1997**

Caroline and the Kept Man

Del brings one of Richard's paintings to a posh country club to impress a girl, but then wealthy socialite Gina Pennetti Schmidt (Ann Magnuson, of *Anything But Love*), who finds Richard with one of his works, may be more taken with the artist than with his art, and Richard suspects she wants to keep him.

Meanwhile, Caroline decides that charity work, rather than another man, is just what she needs and she begins reading to the elderly, finding to her surprise that her first listener turns out to be Stella (Rose Marie, from the original *Dick Van Dyke Show*, reprising her role from a previous *Caroline* episode), who earlier had sold Caroline her antique desk.

Elsewhere, Annie is getting a kick out of the attention she's receiving from her first television commercial.

writer: **Jeff Abugov**
director: **Andrew Tsao**
airdate: **January 21, 1997**

the episodes

Caroline and the Long Shot

Caroline cheers Richard on when he gets the chance to win big money by making the half-court free-throw shot at a New York Knicks game. Less than skilled at shooting hoops, Richard lets Del and Charlie coach him with their best basketball tips.

An over-eager tabloid reporter (French Stewart, of *Third Rock From the Sun*) is assigned to cover Richard's story, while the New York Knicks' City Dancers provide support for Richard during his moment in center court.

Meanwhile, much to Annie's dismay, her mother is "comforted" by none other than Remo.

writer: **Dottie Dartland**
director: **Will Mackenzie**
airdate: **February 11, 1997**

Caroline and the Dearly Departed

Richard finds himself in a life-or-death predicament when Caroline decides to boost the value of his work by convincing influential art columnist Hilton Traynor (John Glover, of *Love! Valour! Compassion!*, Terrence McNally's Tony Award-winning Broadway play) that Richard is a deceased artist.

The plan backfires when Traynor attends the Karinsky funeral with art dealer Kenneth Arabian (Dan Butler, of *Frasier*, reprising his role from the "Caroline and the Gay Art Show" episode).

Meanwhile, Annie meets a casting director (Brent Jasmer, of *The Bold and the Beautiful*) whom she plans on impressing with her dramatic eulogy.

writer: **Jack Kenny and Brian Hargrove**
director: **James Burrows**
airdate: **February 19, 1997**

the episodes

Caroline and the Getaway

Caroline feels that Annie consistently chooses the men in her life over their friendship, and she challenges Annie to take a girls-only ski trip. But chaos ensues when they take the trip together and both girls find romance at the local ski resort.

Meanwhile, Richard thinks he's met the intellectual girl of his dreams (Jessica Stone), but constant interruptions from Del and Charlie may keep the romance at bay.

writer: **Daniel Henriks**
director: **James Burrows**
airdate: **February 25, 1997**

Caroline and the Monkeys

Caroline, who is trying to face single life bravely, tries her hand at an evening alone on the town. She gets a little coaching from Richard, who is quite familiar with a "table for one."

Meanwhile, Annie can't shake her crazy friend Cassandra (Helen Slater, of *City Slickers*, among others), who says she's fine after being released from a sanitarium, but whose dark side resurfaces when Annie introduces her to the unsuspecting Del. Elsewhere, Charlie becomes even wackier than usual, turning paranoid when he's the only one who sees monkeys on the streets of Manhattan.

writer: **Donald Todd**
director: **Andrew Tsao**
airdate: **March 11, 1997**

Caroline and the Buyer

When Caroline supports Del in his effort to expand business for her "Caroline in the City" cartoon strip and merchandise, she doesn't realize that her Midwestern charm has misled Del's new prospective buyer, Bob Anderson (George Segal, of *Just Shoot Me*, among others), into thinking that Caroline is offering to sell more than just her drawings.

Meanwhile, Annie is at her wit's end with her visiting mother (Candice Azzara), although Richard seems to bask in the glow of Mrs Spadaro's motherly love.

writer: **Jeff Abugov**
director: **Will Mackenzie**
airdate: **April 1, 1997**

the episodes

Caroline and the New Neighbor

Caroline's naive, helpful nature comes out in full bloom when she starts catering to her new elderly neighbor, Miriam (Marilyn Cooper, a Tony Award winner for *Woman of the Year*), but Annie thinks Caroline is being taken advantage of.

Later, when Miriam's husband, Walter (Phil Leeds, of *The Larry Sanders Show*, among others), dies, Annie and Caroline are put to the test as Miriam's requests increase.

Meanwhile, appearances can be deceiving when Richard has trouble trying to sell his antique car and ends up getting taken for a ride by a blind man (Steve Paymer, of *Boston Common*).

writer: **Christopher Fife**
director: **Michael Zinberg**
airdate: **April 8, 1997**

Caroline and the Critics

When Caroline discovers that the newspaper in a small upstate New York hamlet hasn't renewed her cartoon strip, she obsesses on the cancellation until she resolves to face the editors in person, convincing a reluctant Richard to join her on a spontaneous road trip.

Meanwhile, Annie is so hurt by an unfair review of one of her stage performances that she vows to seek revenge on the heartless theater critic (Ray Birk).

writers: **Dottie Dartland, Brian Hargrove, Jack Kenny,**
       Tom Leopold and Bill Prady
director: **Will Mackenzie**
airdate: **April 15, 1997**

the episodes

Caroline and the Ombudsman

Caroline has difficulty confronting her neglectful building superintendent, Mr Tedescu (Brian George), about her faulty plumbing, so she hires a mediator, Tom (Bobby Costanzo), to pressure the super into taking care of her request. Later, Caroline panics when she suspects that her "ombudsman" may be a hit man.

Meanwhile, a disenchanted Annie celebrates a milestone theatrical performance in *Cats*, but she later proves that her acting skills are still top-notch when she helps a theater fan (Alan Oppenheimer) repair his tenuous marriage.

writer: **Bill Prady**
director: **Will Mackenzie**
airdate: **April 22, 1997**

Caroline and the Bad Trip

Caroline is thrilled when her agent lands her an appearance on *The Tonight Show* with Jay Leno, and she takes Annie along for the trip to Los Angeles. But Caroline runs into trouble when she accidentally absorbs a questionable substance in the taxi on the way to her big television debut.

Meanwhile, Richard's mother, Natalie (Elizabeth Ashley, reprising her role), makes a quick stop in New York to reveal who Richard's real father was. Elsewhere, Charlie thinks that he has finally found his real father (Bill Daily, of *I Dream of Jeanie*, among others), too, after consulting an adoption agency, while Del tries to teach Richard how to pick up women, with less than successful results, but Richard's future seems a little brighter when he unexpectedly runs into his former one true love, Julia (Sofia Milos, of *Café Americain*).

writer: **Donald Todd**
director: **Michael Zinberg**
airdate: **May 6, 1997**

the episodes

Caroline and Richard & Julia

Richard is stunned when his former love Julia informs him that she is about to be married. To further complicate matters of the heart, Richard convinces Caroline to pretend that she is his wife.

Meanwhile, Annie lands a part in a television show in Los Angeles, and before long begins playing the role of a true starlet, leaving Caroline wondering if she's lost her best friend forever. Elsewhere, Del is convinced that his business is going under and he must sell his beloved Porsche.

writer: **Bill Masters**
director: **Will Mackenzie**
airdate: **May 13, 1997**

Caroline and the Wayward Husband

In the second season's finale cliffhanger: it's the moment of truth in the ongoing charade of Caroline pretending that she and Richard are married – *Bedtime!* – and of course Richard is a wreck.

When Julia and Richard share a romantic moment, Caroline is forced to face her true feelings for Richard.

Meanwhile, in Hollywood, Amy begins work on her new television show with co-star Shadoe Stevens (guest-starring as himself), but her skills as an actress are not exactly entertaining. Elsewhere, in a meeting with his larger-than-life father, King Cassidy (Chad Everett), Del discusses his financial future.

writer: **Kim Friese**
director: **Will Mackenzie**
airdate: **May 20, 1997**

the guest stars

The first two seasons of Caroline have seen a steady parade of guest stars, many of them from other TV series. A partial list follows:

Floyd brings flowers

Morey Amsterdam as Vic in "Caroline and the Watch"
Julie Andrews as herself in "Caroline and Victor/Victoria"
Elizabeth Ashley as Richard's mom in "Caroline and Richard's Mom" and again in "Caroline and the Bad Trip"
Robby Benson as himself in "Caroline and the Movie"
Joseph Bologna as Lou Spadaro, Annie's father in "Caroline and the Ex-Wife"
W. Earl Brown as Floyd the Forest Ranger in "Caroline and the Therapist"
Dan Butler as gallery owner Kenneth Arabian in "Caroline and the Gay Art Show" and again in "Caroline and the Dearly Departed"
John Byner as himself in "Caroline and the Comic"
Jack Carter as himself in "Caroline and the Comic"
Chad Everett as King Cassidy, Del's father, in "Caroline and the Wayward Husband"
Joely Fisher as Del's ex-wife in "Caroline and the Ex-Wife"
John Glover as art columnist Hilton Traynor in "Caroline and the Dearly Departed"
Lauren Graham as Richard's annoying girlfriend Shelly, in several episodes
Mariette Hartley as Caroline's mom in "Caroline and the Twenty-Eight-Pound Walleye"
Judd Hirsch as Richard's dad in "Caroline and the Comic"
Earl Holliman as Caroline's dad in "Caroline and the Twenty-Eight-Pound Walleye"
John Landis as himself in "Caroline and the Movie"
Sharon Lawrence as the recently divorced employment counselor in "Caroline and the Proposal"

Jane Leeves as Daphne in "Caroline and the Bad Back"

Jay Leno as himself in "Caroline and the Bad Trip"

Vicki Lewis as a pushy corporate executive in "Caroline and the Cereal"

Lorna Luft as the travel agent in "Caroline and the Christmas Break"

Rose Marie as Stella in "Caroline and the Watch" and again in "Caroline and the Kept Man"

Michael McKean as Father Damian in "Caroline and the Wedding"

Sofia Milos as Julia, Richard's first love, beginning in "Caroline and the Bad Trip"

Matthew Perry as Chandler in "Caroline and the Folks"

Mackenzie Phillips as Donna Spadaro, Annie's sister, in "Caroline and the Singer"

David Hyde Pierce as Niles Crane in "Caroline and the Bad Back" and as IRS agent Jimmy Callahan in "Caroline and the Cat Dancer"

John Ratzenberger as a quirky prospective apartment tenant in "Caroline and Richard's Mom"

George Segal as the buyer who has something extra on his mind in "Caroline and the Buyer"

Jonathan Silverman as Jonathan Eliot in "Caroline and the Folks"

Helen Slater as Annie's crazy friend Cassandra in "Caroline and the Monkeys"

Jean Stapleton as Caroline's Aunt Mary in "Caroline and the Opera"

Shadoe Stevens as himself in "Caroline and the Wayward Husband"

French Stewart as an over-eager tabloid reporter in "Caroline and the Long Shot"

Meshach Taylor as Caroline's flamboyant agent James in "Caroline and the Cereal"

Renee Taylor as Mrs Fox, Richard's grade-school teacher in "Caroline and the Therapist"

Fabiana Udenio as the nude model in "Caroline and the Gift"

The *Caroline* Lines

(Drum roll, please!)

Caroline
You know, you could try being nicer to Del.

Richard
Yeah, and I could watch Tori Spelling play Medea, but life is just too short.

Richard
I'm stuck!

Del
What do you mean?

Richard
I'm stuck. Are you having trouble with "I'm" or "stuck"?

Annie
[Excited]
Show the dress! Show the dress!

Caroline
I went to eight different stores, and there it was ... Back at the first one.

Annie
Okay, who would you rather sleep with, Ross Perot or one of those flying devil monkeys from *The Wizard of Oz*?

Caroline
Boy monkey or girl monkey?

Del
No way, Phil could never afford to buy her those things on what I paid him.

Charlie
Probably bought it with the money he was embezzling.

Del
What?!

Charlie
He was embezzling, skimming off the top, robbing you blind, spanking the monkey. Oh wait, that's something else.

Richard
So, Donna, do you miss Rome?

Donna
Oh, no. All that traffic and noise and pollution, and rude people.

Richard
Oh, I can see why you moved to New York.

Caroline
Sincere amore.

Richard
I know.

Caroline
What about him?

Annie
Married.

Caroline
No ring.

Annie
He's buying over-the-calf socks.

Caroline
So?

Annie
Over-the-calf socks look better when you're dressed because there's no gap between trouser and sock when you cross your legs.
Crew socks look better when you're undressed because you don't look like a dork. Obviously, this guy cares more about what he looks like dressed than undressed, ergo married.

Caroline
Thanks for answering my ad, Mister Monroe.

Monroe
It's just "Monroe." One word, like "Picasso." Or "Cher." Or "Satan!"

Richard
I'm the one doing the mural on the Reisman Building.

Secretary
Oh, right, the painter!

Richard
Uh, artist.

Secretary
What's the difference?

Richard
I don't have to wear a little white hat.

Richard
'Twas the night before Christmas, and all through the house, there were lots of mice playing, 'cause the cat was dead.

Richard
[As Salty jumps into his lap]
How anecdotal. Can you please just make it disappear.

Caroline
I'm sorry. Are you allergic?

Richard
No, I just don't like cats or dogs or anything that runs up to you and pees on your feet when you come home.

141

The *Caroline* Lines

Richard
Does this elevator go straight to hell
or do I switch in the lobby?

Annie
**[explaining why she didn't
go to the opera]**
If I wanted to listen to fat people
scream in Italian, I'd just go home.

Richard
Excuse me. What do you people
think I do on my birthday?

Caroline
I don't know. I just assumed you
curled up with a handful of dirt from
your homeland and waited 'til dawn.

Richard
Nope that's New Year's

Annie
If you dreamt about kissing Richard
the only thing it means is that you
had bad clams last night.

Annie
You guys will never guess what
happened last night at *Cats*.

Richard
The Humane Society showed up and
decided to have the cast neutered?

Del
You're Jewish.
Can't you help me out?

Richard
Don't tell me, you want me to
stand outside her window and be
your Cyrano de Berkowitz.

Caroline
Come on Richard. this is fun.
Didn't you ever play travel
games when you were a kid?

Richard
No, my parents fed
me Phenobarbital until we got
wherever we were going.
You don't have any, do you?

Charlie
[on tape]
"Thinking of you."

Charlie
Greeting cards on tape. My idea.

Annie
Have a lobotomy. My idea.

Del
Trust me.
I know lies.
I run a greeting card company.

142

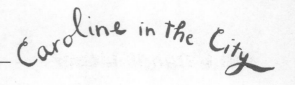

Del

Richard, tell me getting
circumcised doesn't hurt.

Richard

How do I know?
I was eight days old.
I was busy rejecting my
mother's breast.

Del

So Passover is like Easter,
Hanukkah is like Christmas,
and Yom Kippur is like …

Richard

Good Friday without the fun.

Del

Boy, you guys are lucky,
you get a lot of holidays.

Richard

Yeah, it's been a big picnic
the entire five thousand years.

Annie

Wait a minute. You're
pretending you're Jewish
to get a date?

Richard

You've pretended
you were nice to get a date.

Richard

I can't believe you went and
saw my father.

Caroline

Okay, before you yell, I just want you
to know, when I was a child my
parents abandoned me in the
woods and I was raised by a
tribe of busy-bodies.

Richard

**[Richard unchains the door
and Caroline enters]**
If I'd known company was coming I
would've emptied the traps.

Annie

What are you doing?

Richard

I'm going home. The thing you
usually do when you wake up.

Caroline

I don't care if my dry cleaner
doesn't like me any more if my
bank teller likes me.

Richard

I don't think she does.

Caroline

Why, what have you heard?

143

The *Caroline* Quiz

1) By what nickname does Caroline's father call her?
2) What was Caroline's reaction to Del's proposal?
3) After her third break-up with Del, what did Caroline do?
4) What are Del's ex-wives' names?
5) What was the name of Richard's painting that Del thought was so good?
6) Who is Richard's first love?
7) What was the first present Caroline gave Richard?
8) Which artist was Richard's childhood idol?
9) Where is Annie's family from?
10) What was the name of the nerdy guy who borrowed Del's Porsche?
11) What was the name of Annie's ex-convict boyfriend who tried to steal Del's car?
12) What was the name of the employment agency woman with whom Richard had a fling?
13) What was the name of Annie's family dog?
14) What is Salty the cat's real name?
15) What was Shelly's dog's name?
16) What was Annie's understudy's name?
17) Why did Caroline go home to Wisconsin?
18) What was the name of Del's best man at his first two weddings?
19) What was the name of the character that Kenny Williams, Amy Pietz's real-life boyfriend, played in "Caroline and the Bridesmaids"?
20) What was the name of the character that Christine Romeo, Eric Lutes' real-life wife, played in "Caroline and the Bridesmaids"?

Answers

1) Puddin' 2) She got the hiccups 3) She took a weaving class and made Annie a "Del Sucks" bathroom rug 4) Ellen and Jill 5) "My Mother's Womb" 6) Julia 7) A black-and-white cow-shaped pencil sharpener 8) Salvador Dalí 9) Passaic, New Jersey 10) Howie 11) Stephen 12) Maddie Hayward 13) Vandy 14) Tiki 15) Bonnie Belinda 16) Lindsay 17) Because a park was being named after her 18) Greg 19) Eddie 20) Linda